FAWLTY TOWERS
A WORSHIPPER'S COMPANION

LARS HOLGER HOLM

# FAWLTY TOWERS

## A WORSHIPPER'S
## COMPANION

LEO PUBLISHING

*Leo Publishing*
Heleneborgsgatan 44
117 32 Stockholm
Sweden
Telephone/fax: +46 86 69 46 16
E-mail: leopublish@comhem.se
www.leo.infosite.tc

ISBN 91-973661-8-8

Illustrations by the author
Copyright: Lars Holger Holm, 2004
Cover and graphic design: John Eyre

Printed by Preses Nams Corporation
Jana seta printing, Riga 2004

*Thank you Clive, Gilles and Alma for support and inspiration!*

# CONTENTS

# A BLESSING IN DISGUISE

It was toward the end of 2002 that the author of this book began to close in on me in a pincer-like movement. Persistently he had been bombing my agency with ominous epistles – by that time well aware that I do not wish to receive any material related to either Monty Python's Flying Circus or Fawlty Towers – and eventually managed to coerce my manager into such submission that he felt compelled to forward the manuscript. My immediate reaction to it, after having ignored its existence for weeks, was one of genuine indifference. As if that were not enough, I soon also had my long time friend and partner, Bill Morton, on the line, saying he had been contacted by a man who wanted to make sure that I had in fact received his opus with its accompanying letter. I sullenly replied this was the case, but also that I had no idea when, if ever, I would get a chance to read it – and to be sure, I didn't have the slightest intention of doing so. I then buried my head in the sand, hoping the menace would disappear by itself. It did not. Some weeks later the author had Bill forwarding me a fax with the following wording:

*"I am well aware that you are a busy man and that written material of various quality and interest relentlessly keeps adding to the piles in your study. However, beware that Sybil has been dead for quite some*

*time now, so the entire manuscript wrapping her remains is likely to surface quite soon, giving you a last chance to rid yourself of her dead weight and the consequences of your terrible deed ... Let me add on a personal note that* Fawlty Towers – A Worshipper's Companion *involves a very interesting deal for you. Several editors have shown interest in publishing the script, especially after I told them that you would happily contribute with a merry preface to it. I can promise you a handsome percentage of the sales figures if you were to accept this invitation. After all, it is a potential bestseller. Invested with the aura of your fame, your wit and my analytical as well as literary prowess, Dragonfly simply must make it this time! Please, take a look at it. You won't regret it. Then, tell me that you will be more than happy to put your signature under an illustrious preface to this incomparable opus. So take the script now to the 'comfi-chair', open page one and let enjoyment be yours!"*

Realising that the aim of his manouevre was to convince me of writing a preface to a book on a subject that has long since ceased to hold any fascination for me, I felt obliged to tell him the truth: "I apologise that what I am going to say will disappoint you. But I have neither the time nor the motivation to read your book. I have been talking for twenty-five years about Fawlty Towers now, and I would not be at all disappointed if it went away and I could forget about it forever. I am sorry that I can't be more helpful, but I have four projects of my own at present, all of which take up practically every moment that I have. Besides, there are many things that I want to read before I die, which are of higher importance to me than a book, no matter how good, about something I did twenty-five years ago." In essence this was the message I finally faxed to the writer, adding that I was of course delighted that people (such as the author himself) continue to enjoy it, but also that my interest in it beyond that was long gone. I concluded by committing to the 'uncommittal'. "Forgive my being so direct, but I'd rather be quite honest with you. I wish you every success in your endeavours to get a deal."

Still, the peremptory nature of his nonetheless funny, cheerful and, as it eventually turned out, strangely premonitory letter kept haunting me. Then one night I actually dreamt that Sybil (not Prunella Scales!) was dead. But that wasn't all. I had murdered her and I was trying to make money off her in an insurance scam. As I woke up – bathing in sweat, scratching my head – I turned around to my terrified wife with the words: "Sybil, Sybil – what a terrible dream!" Coming to my senses again, it began to dawn on me that whatever crimes we have committed in the past, there is no way we will ever escape them, and the surest way to become the unwilling prey of that same past, is to deny it its rightful place in our present lives. For me, Fawlty Towers belongs to a painful, confused, not to say disturbed, period of my life. It involved such an effort that I almost ended up in a mental asylum, and I dare say that if it hadn't been for the vast quantities of Prozac I was prescribed during my 'convalescence', I don't think I would ever had got over and beyond it. Today, I feel happy and relieved that the problems dealt with in the series are no longer of my concern, but when I finally, in a sense of obligation toward myself, actually started to read Mr. Holm's manuscript, I fortunately realised that the subject of his writing was no longer of my doing; it was a creation which, like Frankenstein's monster, had taken an appearance of its own in order to continue its work of destruction in the world.

Lars Holger Holm's book on Fawlty Towers is in my opinion pretty close to a nightmare come true. It pleases me to be able to add, though, that it is also, simultaneously, an incredibly well written and witty book, which, in its delightful blend of farce and profundity, will above all please anyone sufficiently neurotic and tormented to see a role model in that most twisted of human characters named Basil Fawlty. I shall consequently not hesitate to re-commend the book to anyone interested in making a thwarted thing even more thwarted. I will likewise – and in order to fore-stall all unwanted attention – seize the opportunity to assure the reader that the facts stated in his book are all correct. There are, of course, a few things that the writer doesn't and can't know any-thing about, but I think that is only proper. Then, so far as it re-mains to be seen if the "handsome percentage" offered to the wri-ter of this preface will in any significant way materialise. If it does, I might even consider releasing on DVD the ruthlessly revealed thirteenth episode, of which I unfortunately still have the original copy. This much I promise. But don't call me, or Bill, and don't send any letters or e-mails. It will only make Sybil suspicious in her grave and my present wife jealous. You see, in spite of my efforts to the contrary, she has never been quite able to convince herself that I actually managed to leave 16, Elmwood Avenue behind for good. Lars Holger Holm, obviously, is of the same opinion. Thus, I have all good reason to fear the spectre of sibylline revenge.


*J.C.*

# INTRODUCTION

THIS GUIDE BOOK ADDRESSES itself to those ardent admirers of Fawlty Towers who have long since left the innocent stage behind when Manuel seemed merely funny, Polly only benevolent, Sybil just acrimonious and Basil plain crazy. It proposes to probe deep, deeper and still deeper into the texture of this work; to reveal intricate codes, hidden staircases and secret chambers; to interpret runes and unravel psychological mysteries. It is a spiritual adventure into the black hole in the centre of a speculative universe in constant expansion; a Gnostic, hermetic, alchemical experiment of rare complexity and eerie fascination. Last but not least, the book seeks to finally put an end to the ludicrous assumptions that there were only twelve episodes in all, that the only Jesus that ever lived died on the cross, and that Hitler committed suicide in the bunker.

On a more mundane level the book can also be used as a kind of dictionary for those who are irritated when unable to tell exactly in which show a specific line originates, or those who feel inadequate and embarrassed when one of Basil's references eludes them. It is expressly and most emphatically dedicated to the *fanatic* who already has all the Towers on video or DVD – perhaps even all the records with Manuel presenting the shows, all the other books, the T-shirt, the jig-saw puzzle, the tea cups and the spppooons! – and yet can not help chuckling with delight every time an episode is aired on TV. To this spectator and reader, – that is, to anyone who recognises and appreciates the fact that a reference, like a Russian doll, may hide another reference hiding yet another one – the present work will be of immense, not to say immeasurable, value, as well as a constant source of joy and entertainment.

To secure the greatest benefit from the many analyses and reflections following this brief introduction, the reader, who for some reason or other does not meet with the above-mentioned qualifications, is well advised to refresh his memory of 'all' twelve episodes. It will also be expected that he keeps to hand a copy of the printed script to the shows (can be bought or ordered at the best book shops – *Guild Publishing* sponsored me for adding this last line, so bear with me: it *had* to be there …). Assuming the last exhortation to be superfluous to any Real Fawlty Devotee (RFD), I shall no longer keep anyone in suspense but press on with my task. First I turn to the dramatis personae themselves. As we get to know them they are all guests, staff or owners at the Towers. Each also has a past, albeit, perhaps, not much of a future. But as I'm sure that the merry spectator has always been eager to know what the Major really did during the war, and how on earth radiant Polly ended up in stuffy old Torquay, I have the honour and the privilege to present:

# 1

# THE CONDENSED BIOGRAPHIES OF THE INHABITANTS OF FAWLTY TOWERS

# THE MAJOR

MAJOR GOWEN WAS BORN in 1904 in the county of Sussex in a small village half-way between Tunbridge Wells and East Grinstead. He was the second son of parents who, although they were of modest means, nevertheless considered themselves rich indeed in their veneration of the Royal family. It was only natural that young Henry Gowen, ever respectful of his parents' wishes, from an early age should consider it incumbent upon him to go out and help govern India.

After leaving school he was admitted to the Military Academy at Sandhurst, at which establishment his singular lack of military aptitude was at once, and generally, recognised – though all who thought they remembered him also testify to his benign and equable disposition. Gowen finally passed out of the Academy in 1926 – there was still a dearth of subalterns, the result of the slaughter of the First World War, so pass-marks were perhaps somewhat relaxed – to become a soldier at last. He was at once, and in accordance with his ardent wish, posted to India.

During his service on the subcontinent, Gowen's military exploits made little impression on any that happened to be subjected to them, Indians and Sahibs alike. Needless to add, it became a matter of principle to him not to pick up more than a few scattered phrases from any 'native' language. This proved to be a wise pre-

caution, as it did effectively prevent others from realising his constitutional inability to produce even the guttural sounds of Indian dialects. In addition, he was conveniently convinced that an Englishman who condescended to the language of natives was betraying his nation and, in doing so, civilisation per se. Nonetheless, Gowen was to pay his tribute to India by perfecting his one indubitable accomplishment, a stunning imitation of the roar of a tiger. His propensity for demonstrating this particular talent at inopportune moments, however – the District Commissioner's garden party is a case in point – somewhat detracted from its entertainment value, and indeed, as time wore on, from its novelty.

When the British Raj, in agreement with the government back home, finally felt that the time had come for old Britannia to pass on the sceptre she had herself once seized from the hands of the last Moghul emperor and to grant India independence, Gowen was seconded to England on 'special duties' of a nature so secret that he never did discover what they actually were. Repatriated after nearly fifteen years in the tropics, Gowen, paradoxically, found himself rather unoccupied in the very opening stages of another war. He also found himself thinking more and more often of the redemptive power of the love of a good woman. But in spite of his no doubt sincere intentions to find one, he proposed marriage to a French girl, rumoured to have connections with the Resistance. His proposal was fatefully accepted, a fact that in later years would induce him to speak of the lady as having been rather, and somewhat perfidiously, a member of the 'lack of resistance' – he would always refer to this as his best joke, and fearful of forgetting it, made sure to tell it as often as possible.

His beloved, unaccustomed to the charms of tea and crumpets, proved to be immune to the seductive qualities of slippers, cardigans and pipe-smoking by the fire, and, in making off with a proportion of the gallant soldier's savings, became something of a disappointment to him. The lady's younger sister, to whom he then turned – having high hopes of initiating her into the mysteries of cricket – likewise proved unsatisfactory, absconding with his wallet during the course of a test match. Twice-bitten and thrice-shy, but unembittered, the Major resumed a bachelor existence. He never remarried.

Some years into the war, Captain Gowen, although eager to do his duty for Queen and country, was removed by his superiors even farther away from the principal field of action, and sent to join a detachment of superannuated warriors somewhere in the north of England. In this remote and peaceful area he uncomplainingly served out his time until happening to read in the morning newspaper one day that the war was over. (He has, as we know, been mildly obsessed with newspapers ever since.)

Such was Captain Gowen's military history, then, in an attempt to forestall the difficulties in finding him an adequate post-war assignment, his masters decided to remove him from what might loosely be termed 'active service', and bade him a honourary farewell as a Major. He was never to adopt another career.

His modest army pension afforded him little in the way of luxury, so he sold his flat and left London. He moved thence to Eastbourne, where he lived in the seafront hotel East Eden until its proprietor, in a fit of absent-mindedness, burnt it to the ground. He then moved westward along the coast, searching for some quiet backwater blessed with a benign microclimate, surrounded by emerald-green golf courses. He was eventually washed up, like a crab in a tide's end pool, in Basil Fawlty's stagnant domain. Here Major Gowen has come to rest, the only apparent reminiscensces of his former life being the daily battle cry, "Papers arrived yet, Fawlty?" and the gin-and-tonics he imbibes in quantities calculated sufficient to stave off the occasional malarial attack.

# POLLY SHERMAN - THE HANDY GIRL

POLLY FIRST SAW THE light of day in Kansas City in 1950. In her earliest years her greatest wish was to become a film star. Like so many other young hopefuls she headed west to California, then at the height of flower power. She had a letter of introduction to the fairly famous producer Max Holger, who arranged a screen test for her. This, alas, most incontrovertibly proved that she could no more act, dance or sing than she could fly to the moon. Ambition undimmed, Polly decided that her real future was in live theatre. She moved from the west to the east coast, specifically to New York, took a job as a waitress in a Brooklyn diner, and enrolled in theatre classes. Her conspicuous lack of acting talent was immediately recognised by her tutors, and made brutally clear to her. But Polly, ever optimistic, interpreted this to mean that her real vocation was to become, not a Broadway artist, but a Shakespearean actress, and that there was nothing for it but to come to the U. K., where her gifts would be immediately obvious to all.

She worked day and night, poor girl, to raise the money for the fare to London, only to find on her arrival in England that the London theatre was every bit as competitive as that of New York. Polly came to her senses at last; she turned to art and literature, hoping to become a successful painter or playwright. Her drawing

skills were happily superior to her histrionic abilities, and she won a place at Goldsmith's College.

By the end of her second term Polly was out of funds. The college authorities had pronounced themselves sufficiently satisfied with her progress, and would award her a grant at the beginning of the autumn term. Meanwhile the long vacation was approaching, and she could not afford to keep her flat over the summer months. What to do? She had after all come a considerable way, and was happy in London, but there weren't many jobs to be had in the city.

She was looking at the Jobs Vacant boards at the employment centre one morning when an advertisement on the Out-of-Town board caught her attention. It read "Female assistant required in clean and respectable hotel on the English Riviera. Contact Mr. Basil Fawlty, Fawlty Towers. Note: No bleeding pets or boyfriends on the premises." There was a telephone number. Polly decided to give it a try, and was lucky, or unlucky, to speak to Sybil rather than Basil.

She went down to Torquay on the coach. Upon her arrival she met with and was interviewed by Sybil. Basil, strolling by, took a look down Polly's nicely filled decolletage, and without reference to or further discussion with Sybil, hired her on the spot. To avenge herself for this affront Sybil offered to pay only half her travelling expenses, although Basil said he would reimburse her in full. Surprisingly enough, he did honour his promise. Sybil must never know, of course.

This simple gesture of decency, signifying more to Polly than the act itself warranted, turned out to be Basil's best deal ever. In fact, those few extra pounds were to prove an astonishingly cheap, automatically renewed full-coverage life insurance policy. It was a life-saver, his buffer against the apparently random hostilities emanating from people and things in his surroundings. Simply by for once keeping his word, Basil was blessed with the presence of a fairy; from then on, and for ever after, Basil could always, or almost always, count on Polly's loyalty whenever he got himself into serious trouble.

This was the way things stood when Polly set foot in Fawlty Towers' reception that summer. It didn't take long for her to realise that whatever her hopes or fears had been, she could say goodbye to them now, since the world she had entered was situated in the twilight zone. She was never able to explain the powerful attraction it exerted on her, but she really was an artist insofar as the imaginary and the real, for her as well, tended to blend in one single vision.

Did she feel sorry for Basil? Perhaps. Did she want to get out of it all? Certainly. But the force that kept her posted was stronger than her own will. After all, the delusive prospect of a career as an actress had driven her all the way to England. Capable of submitting herself to a grandiose illusion, Fawlty Towers, contrary to what one might naturally expect, did not represent a madhouse pure and simple to her. Yet, she had only come to stay and to help out during the summer. All of a sudden she realised she had been there for five years …

# MANUEL GOMEZ - THE SPANISH WAITER

MANUEL WAS BORN IN Barcelona in May 1947, or was it October 1948? Mother was never quite sure. Incontrovertible, however, is that Manuel was one of a family of eleven siblings – or perhaps only ten. In May 1947 his mother and the rest of the family had been so preoccupied with mourning the deceased father – said to have passed away with an expression of profound relief on his face – that she hardly had time to register another childbirth. Rumour has it that one of the siblings actually snapped the child from the cradle and sold him for folding money in the street. The baby boy disappeared for many months, but was rediscovered in a nearby hospital where he was used in demonstrations to young bourgeois mothers of how to change nappies and take temperatures.

In October 1948 another family crisis reared its head. Although Father had been dead for over a year and Mother had never re-married, she nevertheless found herself about to give birth for the eleventh time – or perhaps only tenth – a fact which she had tried to hide for as long as possible, suspecting one of her sons of having taken advantage of her during the siesta. Mother consequently found it hard to look this latest addition to the family in the face. In addition, Manuel and his brother Pepe did look surprisingly identical, just like twins. A famous Spanish doctor, who once observed them, became interested in the anomaly and wanted to make a case out of an exceptional twin birth where one foetus had been arrested in its development and waited for his brother to get ready and out of the womb, before he himself started to grow. But it had all been speculation. In reality, Manuel never knew whether his father was a man he had never seen, buried in the very same month as he was born, or one of his brothers. And since Manuel never really knew who his father was, he could never be quite sure who he was himself.

Over time a Dickensian aura of faithful love not reciprocated would spread around Manuel. He continued to revere his mother although she hardly took any notice of him. He was in fact a notably good-natured boy; the problem was that he was also, to say the least, very clumsy. In due course he learned both to read and write, but didn't care overmuch for either activity, as, in his hands, objects like books and pens assumed characteristics not normally associated with such peaceful artefacts, and tended to wound him and anyone else who happened to be in their vicinity.

However, an obliging nature can compensate for many other shortcomings in this world, and at the age of nine Manuel found a job with a bakery. Somehow the building caught fire during the course of his first morning on the job, and Manuel was blamed for the conflagration.

From this point onwards, Manuel's career took a turn for the even worse. Although he was always eager to learn, he was nonetheless considered impossible to educate, and he soon acquired hierostratic fame in all of Barcelona for his remarkable capacity of turning a flourishing local business enterprise into a disaster within a week. In order to get this human earthquake out of town for good, a group of concerned citizens put together a dazzling recommendation to the Foreign Office, the principal agency governing temporary employment outside Spain but within the European Economic Community. The authorities looked through their files of vacancies and found an obscure hotel on the south-west coast of England. In Devon, of all places. Wasn't that where Sir Francis Drake came from, the bandido? "Help needed?" *Hola Ingles*: "We'll send you help all right!" The only condition is that you pay for the transportation of the subject; otherwise you can have him for as long as you like …

Talk about killing two birds with one stone. By this seemingly innocuous act Barcelona was not only to rid herself of her most prodigiously dangerous son, but also, on behalf of all of Spain, to avenge the debacle of the Armada outside Cadíz once and for all.

Time for the *estocado. Olé*!

# MISS TIBBS AND MISS GATSBY -
# THE LADIES

THE ORIGINS OF THE Ladies go back to times so shrouded in legend that they themselves have difficulty in recalling the name of the king that was on the throne at the time of their angelic church-bell-accompanied descent from the blessed meadows of female compassion. Although to an uninitiated eye it must seem as if the Ladies have never once been apart, a quick glance in their old diaries and withered letters would confirm that they did meet for the first time in London sometimes in the early 1930s, and that over the years they became quite inseparable in working for the cause dearest to their hearts: the welfare of the poor. Like the Major they remained in the line of duty until they became eligible for state pension, and neither ever married.

Violet Tibbs spent her early years and youth in Rhodesia – as the area now encompassing the countries of Zimbabwe and Zambia was then called. One calamitous day a dashing young man from Cape Province was introduced to her. She immediately fell passionately in love with him, but her family, over which a stout British patriarch held sway, did not approve of the fellow, reputed to be nothing more than a gambler, womaniser and all-round bounder.

Violet's elopement with the rapscallion led, after some exciting travel adventures, to bitterness and sorrow, for quite apart from being disinherited and shunned by her family, she lost her lover

too. Calculating that no more money was to be wrung from his fiancée, the confidence trickster turned his attentions to other, more profitable sources of income – wealthier women, in fact.

Violet was left behind in London in disgraceful circumstances – she was poor as a church mouse and pregnant. But she was too afraid to attempt a termination (a risky undertaking in those days), so the child was actually brought into this world. Some English relatives eventually gave her food and shelter, but forced her to give the child up for adoption. She was never to see her son again. Soon after his birth she tried to commit suicide, thinking that a bottle of gin spiced up with sufficient quantities of bromide would be enough to send her back to her maker. It wasn't. It just sent the bromural and the alcohol back onto the bedspread, and she herself into a tremendous hangover.

Violet found it hard to ever get over her first and unhappy love, which had been sincere on her side. However, she had by now accepted her fate. Although other men would court and even propose to her (she was a beautiful woman in her youth and remained striking well into the autumn of her life), she never accepted any hand in marriage and sublimated herself in philanthropy.

On the anniversary of her forty years as a dedicated social worker, a merry farewell party was organised in her honour at the Social Service headquarters (the so-called SS) and a week later she was to receive from the chairman's hand the charity medal for merit of the first order. That day was a happy one for Miss Tibbs. She sat at the chairman's table for high tea, she was surrounded by colleagues and officials who all wanted to shake hands, or even embrace her. But best of all was that from now one she would enjoy a much deserved retirement.

Together with Miss Gatsby, with whom she had been sharing a flat in Earls Court, she decided to retire to the countryside, preferably somewhere close to the sea. They spent a week at Fawlty Towers in Torquay one summer and found themselves well taken care of by the staff, which at that time included the faithful old, and in a Swedenborgian sense, clairvoyant servant Elsie, who later used to conduct spiritual seances in their rooms, read tarot cards and join the Ladies for bingo after church on Sundays.

When the Ladies found out that the pension also offered rooms for standing residents, they simply decided to move their whereabouts. When we meet them, they have been there for the last nine years, almost as long as the Major himself, and with whom verbal exchange has advanced to conversational subtleties such as: "Good morning Major." "Good morning Ladies, nice day, isn't it?"[1]

Miss Rose Gatsby's story is more commonplace but perhaps also a bit sadder than that of her dear friend, for where Violet had deliberately chosen, after her one disastrous relationship, to become a spinster, there had in Rose's case really not been much of a choice. Born into a middle-class Lancashire family as the youngest of three daughters, she seemed destined to remain the white spot on the map. Although the father was solicitous for all his daughters, he only managed to successfully marry off the two oldest. When Rose turned thirty-five years of age, she herself lost heart. At the same time her father fell seriously ill. Rose, still living with her parents, felt that it was her duty to help her old mother to nurse him. He died the same year and Rose mourned him piously.

It is possible that she also loved other men, but they were never to know. Over the years Rose, contrary to her real nature, had grown shy and taciturn. It was only when she finally met Violet that she dared to speak of her fears and insecurities. However, by that time it was too late to get married. When her mother died as well, Rose finally decided to make an attempt to lead a life of her own. She used the money bequeathed by her father to come to London and open a small hatshop in Earls Court. Having little flair for fashion she failed to make a profit. Violet, living nearby, had walked past the shop many times. Early one evening the sign

---

[1] I am aware that there is some controversy as to whether or not the Ladies have been inhabitants of the Towers for a longer period of time than the Major. In The Wedding Party Basil introduces the Major to Mrs. Peignoir with the qualification that he is "our longest-standing resident." On the other hand we have Miss Tibbs informing Sybil in the The Kipper and the Corpse that "we (she and Miss Gatsby) are his (Basil's) oldest residents." It is possible that this should not be interpreted to mean that they are the hotel's longest-standing residents, but only the ones most advanced in age. Accepting this hypothesis I am inclined to confer upon the Major the honour of having first discovered and settled in the Towers for good.

announcing its liquidation caught her eye and prompted her to take a peep inside. She walked in and found Rose alone in the empty room, weeping. Violet took her home to tea and Chelsea buns, and told her about the peace of mind that charity work had brought her. Little by little Rose cheered up, and when Violet firmly concluded that there is always someone worse off than oneself, Rose had already been on the track on which she was to remain for a good thirty years. In other words, Violet talked her into becoming a charity woman, just like herself. From this point onwards, Rose slowly and steadily regained confidence in herself, and it was often noticed how well they complemented each other in diverse situations, the persistence and benign patience of Rose forming a natural counterpart to the sanguine humour and vivacity of Violet.

And it wasn't Miss Tibbs who founded their common treasury. Starting with the little money left from her own inheritance, Miss Gatsby, practical and with foresight as always, began to save small amounts from their monthly salaries and place them in government bonds. A mere five weeks after Violet received her gold medal, and her pension, Rose decided that she was not going to wait for her own medal, since the national lottery, in which the Ladies participated once a year through their possession of bonds, had meanwhile opened its gates to them and rewarded their unselfish zeal in service of the under-privileged with the handsome sum of £50.000.

Violet, ever fearful of the vengeance of her long-dead father, urged Rose to give the better part of it away to charity, to set up a foundation in their name or something. Rose not only contradicted her friend, but decided that enough was enough. They had given most of their lives to further the welfare of the riff-raff, now it was time for them to live for themselves, and to enjoy it.

Rose argued that there was absolutely nothing wrong in keeping the money as long as they did not flaunt it. They would remain true to their modest ways, all the same knowing that they could always allow themselves a little luxury every now and then … Over time, this added luxury tended to manifest itself in two rather voluminous wardrobes, and a rich collection of pearls, necklaces and bracelets. But these items were slowly amassed and did not even arouse the suspicion of Sybil, who must have concluded that the Ladies had been given these jewels at various stages of their lives, perhaps even by various admirers, now passed away.

Nobody knew that they were keeping a fortune inside their own mattresses, and it would probably never have become known if it weren't for the fact that the charitable disposition of the Ladies was to be called upon one last time – in a real life-and-death situation. Needless to add, the Ladies responded to the challenge by once again rising to the heroic heights of true Englishness, where material things, such as money, and again money, are invariably sacrificed for a higher cause …

# TERRY - THE ALLEGED KITCHEN CHEF

TERRY SEEMED DESTINED TO become a criminal of one sort or another. Born to neglectful parents in a desolate South London housing estate, he was obliged at an early age to join his local street gang, the Friends of Chaos. These young men spent most of their time defending their turf from incursions by rival gangs such as the Borough Street Boys, the Fierce Meerkats and the Siberian Hamsters.

Terry grew up to be neither particularly strong nor tall, but he was agile, and competent in his use of knife and boot. He rose quickly through the ranks of the Friends, partly because of his skills, partly on account of his charm and sociopathic tendencies, so indispensable in making one's way in the hierarchy of gang life. In fact, his popularity was such that he became a prized target of neighbouring gangs, much as a famed Aztec warrior was sought out in battle for capture and sacrifice.

One evening he was attacked and severely beaten, regaining consciousness some time later to find a visiting-card neatly pinned to the lapel of his fancy stolen leather jacket. "Congratulations," it read, "You have just had a full and frank exchange of views with the Siberian Hamsters." His watch was on his wrist, his wallet and stash of drug-samples untouched. After a couple of weeks of fairly careful nursing, Terry was taken to court, convicted of possessing drugs with intent to supply, and sent to prison, where his life was to undergo a dramatic change.

His cell-mate turned out to be the enormously erudite art historian and former Cistercian brother Mark Whistlebourne, who had ended up behind bars because he had been unable to keep his expertise in forging master works by Rembrandt, Turner and Cezanne to himself. On the contrary, he had made himself a handsome fortune by providing insatiable art collectors and museums all over the world with a number of strikingly inauthentic masterpieces. When Terry got to know about his astonishing career he began striking up conversations, for instance by asking if it was diffcult to learn the trade of art forgery. "Well, if you want quick results, go for Fauviste works; they are all fake anyway."

However, during pottery class one afternoon the master-forger confided to Terry that he was seriously considering a change of career, and going straight. He had amassed enough money to buy a flat in Brighton, where he would be among friends, and besides, a spot of honesty would make a nice change – at least for a while. "I've never wallowed in the luxury of a perfectly blameless bourgeois existence," he told Terry. "It's time to give it a bash."[2] In expansive mood still, he advised Terry to think about doing the same.

Mr. Whistlebourne's advice stayed in Terry's memory. On his release from prison, and with the help of the Prisoners' Aid

---

[2] Ironically, Mr. Whistlebourne's conversion to decency did not occur quite in the way he had prefigured it. Upon his release from prison, he was immediately contacted by the management of the Tate Gallery, which had recently lost substantial sums of money – and prestige – by first buying inauthentic masterpieces and then trying to track down the forgers themselves. In order to spare the museum these inconveniences in the future, someone had come up with the brilliant idea of hiring Mr. Whistlebourne, the greatest expert of them all, on the techniques of forgery. Mark Whistlebourne accepted the job and soon became so famous that he was also asked by the BBC to do his own series, in which he divulged to the television viewers the secrets of producing hitherto unknown Turner and Monet paintings …

Society, Terry obtained a place at a catering school. He found that he had something of an affinity for the work, left the school with creditable marks, and took the first of a series of short-order jobs (fish and chips mainly). It was a major promotion for him when he was chosen from a shortlist of three to be second chef at a small hotel in Dorchester. Here he stayed for five years or so, gainfully and on the whole happily employed, till the hotelier retired, and the new regime proved not to his taste.

Terry's attention was drawn to an advertisement placed in the tourist pamphlet *What's on in Torquay?* by the Fawltys, whose previous chef had been asked to leave after unaccountably trying to

strangle Manuel in the kitchen. Basil had been very understanding, not to say happy, about the chef's reaction and intent, but
one of the guests during that lunch hour had happened to be a
high-ranking police officer off duty, and this gentleman suddenly
felt that it was his duty to return to duty and to file a report.

Terry was given the job on three months' approval. "We have
to make sure that you don't kill the guests before we can give you
the job more permanently," Basil succinctly outlined the situation.
Terry felt insulted, of course, but then he too had seen some
ruffians in his day. Born and bred cockney, he would never convince Mr. Fawlty about his own discerning taste. But it didn't matter so much, since the assumption of social superiority in Basil
himself was, after all, more often than not, affected.

# BASIL FAWLTY -
# OWNER AND MANAGER AS WELL

IT WOULD BE NATURAL to assume that a person as singular as Basil Fawlty must come from a family of extraordinary eccentrics. Truth to tell, this is not the case. His father, a kindly and somewhat taciturn figure, used to work as Ombudsman (although the title was conferred upon him retroactively, since not even the Swedes had come up with it at that early date) for the Transport and General Workers' Union in Swanage. In other words, his father was a union representative, and we may get a first-hand impression of Basil's contempt for his own old man by noting the strange mixture of frustration and fury he displays when later in life the name of Harold Wilson, the late Labour Party leader, is mentioned in his presence.

From a very early age, Basil found nothing so odious in life as trade unions, and we would do well to remind ourselves that his father was not only a member of such an organisation, but an important official, a spider in the web, which in Basil's view practically turned him into a traitor of his country, perhaps even into a communist ... To complete the picture we must add the presence of a complacent, loving mother, doing embroidery, ironing shirts, cooking meals. And then there is, contrary to all expectation, Basil's younger brother, all in all a little group which to any innocent eye would appear to be the very image of reliable, honest middle-class

family peacefully striving towards social justice and weekends enjoyed having picnics on the miniscule lawn in front of their respectable semi.

As soon as he was old enough to leave home for good, Basil's brother, Leslie, emigrated to Australia. He used to write or call about once or twice a year to his parents but he never included Basil in their communications, and the inevitable conclusion is that something must have happened between Basil and his younger brother during their childhood or adolescent years that permanently estranged them.

There is no lack of diverse and quite plausible grounds for how this came to happen. One very probable explanation is that Basil, in adminstering the rites of passage that every older brother has a duty to impose on his younger male siblings, overdid it. There is for instance a case in point that dates from the brothers' teenage years. Leslie had received a beautiful model sports car on his birthday and would give demonstrations of its wonders to anyone who seemed inclined to marvel at them. Basil's reaction was at first to show envy, but this uneasy feeling quickly turned into scheming of sinister portent. For where your average elder brother might go so far as to, by accident as it were, remove the steering-wheel, Basil opened up the roof with his mother's sturdiest tin-opener, fastened it back down with a sardine-tin key, and presented Leslie with a neatly typed bill for the installation of a sun-roof of the very latest design.

Also, at school, Basil was considered odd on account of his many idiosyncrasies. Basil in his turn not only despised his family, but his schoolmates as well, with the result that neither the school nor his parents made any effort to help him go to university, though this was his dream. But, alas, he hadn't attended boarding school at Eton or elsewhere, he was an ordinary public-school student, and the school refused to help him, in spite of his talent, since the day when he in a fit of rage publicly declared that they (the headmaster, the staff and the pupils) were all unmitigated riff-raff, and not even worthy of tying his shoelaces.

Basil of course never got the money or the grades to complete his transference from the antechamber of the Swanage Transport Union to the elect fraternity of scholars. He had always wanted to study, and considered himself apt for it. Maybe he was in a sense lucky in never having to be put to the test. On the other hand, from now on he would begin considering himself a superior man held back by the monumental ignorance and envy of his fellow men. At the same time he had to take all kinds of jobs where his superiors seldom missed a chance to make fun of his seigneurial manners and scholarly pretensions, in this way fatally fuelling his ardent desire for revenge …

# SYBIL FAWLTY - BASIL'S WIFE

THEN CAME THE DAY when Basil first met Sybil. Oh, it all seemed so right, didn't it? There she was, in a corner of the pub with her female hairdresser colleagues (including Audrey). Basil, awfully shy as always when it came to girls, managed to spill something on Sybil's dress, who, surprised at first, found him touching in his desperate efforts to put it right again. He bought her another drink, they started to talk and, lo and behold (as Sybil later confessed to Audrey) she at first found him both charming, easy(!), attractive and amusing … She realised that he was impractical, but since she had read little beyond fashion, make-up and hair-style articles in the women's weeklys, she was very impressed with Basil's learning and admired him greatly, especially in comparison to the kind of men her friends (notably Audrey) had to put up with.

Sybil's laughter had always been dreadful – an odd mixture of animal bellowing and unarticulated sarcasm – but Basil didn't notice it so much at the early stages of their acquaintance, principally because at the beginning he was always laughing just as much as she was. It was only later that they stopped laughing together, and only after they had married that Basil stopped laughing altogether. Considering Sybil's by no means slight capacity for gossip, it would be natural to assume that during childhood and adolescence she must have had many sisters with whom she was able to exchange confidences. But whereas the assumption in Basil's case was that he must have been an only child, Sybil – once again quite contrary to natural expectation – really was the only child of an Eastbourne dressmaker and an absconder sailor.

The mother had been of somewhat lax morals in her early years, capable of accommodating, over a given period of time, more than one man in her life and bed. However, when she became pregnant with that Canadian rascal, she really wanted to marry him. But the future father, once he had enjoyed the lush warmth of her embrace, ran off like a rat through a sewer and never showed up again, although he had solemnly promised to return to make her and her child respectable and abandon his maritime vagabondage. As a child Sybil was to become painfully aware of how stigmatising it can be to be born out of wedlock, and she dreaded the destiny which had befallen her mother. Although the latter eventually assumed proper responsibility for her child and drastically reduced the number of her casual male acquaintances, she was never able to win full acceptance in society and she was, if not downright frowned upon, at least pitied for remaining unmarried for no good reason. The ladies of high, if not the highest, society were not in the least ashamed of wearing a fancy frock sewn by her hand. But the fact that they appreciated her sewing skills didn't mean that they were ever going to treat her with more respect than mere convention required. Besides, they were jealous. Something told them that she had had more fun in her days than all of them together ever would. In fact, Sybil's mother used to smile even when she was sad, and she had a laugh so loud and eerily penetrating that the fog-horn in the light house by the pier had to be replaced by a signal sounding like a church bell in order to prevent ship crews, approaching the narrowing strait of Dover, from mistaking her voice for a nautical signal.

dry little
nest of
vipers

Sybil went to state school, but only for as long as she had to. She then went to the Young Ladies Academy for Hair Care, passed her examinations and got a job at a beauty parlour in Swanage. At the same time, partly in reaction to the licentiousness of her mother – an over-reaction akin to that of the children of alcoholics – partly as an expression of the need to be respected by a man and by society, Sybil decided that she was never going to accept the fate of her mother, namely, to remain unmarried and be gossiped about because of her innate frivolity.

Sybil was very much like her mother when it came to talking and bragging about all kinds of erotic exploits, and she had good reason to fear that similarity. Once safely married, she reckoned, there was on the other hand nothing to prevent her from keeping up her mother's good work, at least verbally. As we all know, this is exactly what she did, and with great aplomb. Meanwhile appearances must be maintained at all costs. This ambition was soon destined to turn Sybil into a petit-bourgeois player of the worst kind: the *wanna-be* petit bourgeois.

It is easy to see that Sybil probably was just a tiny bit too eager to drag Basil to the altar – a few more months of caution and she might have ended up in a place and a marriage of a different kind. On the other hand, apart from Basil's near-total incompetence in any activity connected to hotel management, he was at least a man and they had – God knows how? – yes, precisely, managed to turn a decrepit B&B into a flourishing money-making machine. That was a fact that spoke for itself and not even Sybil could deny it, but then again she regarded that achievement as practically of her own making, in spite of the difficulties.

And what about Basil himself? Did he ever suspect George of anything? Wasn't it strange that Sybil always had to leave home every time he walked out on Audrey? Basil would never give it a second thought, but there were certainly evil tongues out there that could have filled him in on the rumours, if only he had cared to listen. Not that the rumours had ever been substantiated, still …

Sybil, the dragon, the old trouble and strife, the alpha and omega of his life, was his first woman for real. Was she also to become his last? It never dawned on either of them that a divorce probably would have been the simplest solution to their problems – they belonged to a generation that basically married according to the old-fashioned vow: 'until death hopefully do us part'. And love is a strange and wonderful thing. It is not logical, and Sybil, no matter what, somehow admired Basil even long after they had opened a hotel together, and he was, no matter what, always afraid of her. There have been worse excuses for a marriage.

What was finally the truth of their childlessness; was Sybil unable to get pregnant, or was Basil unable to impregnate her, or was it he or she who didn't want any offspring, or was it simply the combination of the two of them which excluded even the possibility of discussing this option? We shall never know, but we can always speculate.

# THE NEUROSES

2

*"There is enough material there for an entire conference."*

FOR MOST PEOPLE IN this world, an encounter with a real-life Basil would be like meeting a veritable freak of nature, the hotel itself representing the entrance of and reception at Jurassic Park. But just as paleontologists have long since accepted that not only man, but God too must have had some singular nightmares during the course of natural history, the psychologist cannot but detect an unusual variety of potential mental disturbances in Basil Fawlty. The man is a virtual compendium of neuroses. In many ways he can be studied as the embodiment of an entire nation's collective idiosyncrasies, hereditary eccentricities and fatal aberrations. A close study of this rich soul in all its extravagant divergences from the 'acceptable' should therefore give rise to conclusions, not only about Basil, but also about people around him, that are at once insightful, profound, paradoxical and intriguing. Let us therefore begin by specifying the general nature of these disturbances as we discover them, and classifying them under some appropriate headings.[3]

THE CLASS PHOBIA – Basil's irremediable hatred and fear of the *hoi polloi*, and his flirtations with what he sees as high society (see especially the episodes A Touch of Class and Gourmet Night).

THE SEXUAL PHOBIA – Basil's crusade against all forms of sexual desire not once and for all rendered harmless by marriage.

THE RACIAL PHOBIA – A complex problem indeed, exemplified in the exasperated fury that the very sight of Manuel induces in Basil, and in his inability to assimilate the fact that Sybil's ingrowing toe-nail is to be treated by a 'surprisingly' civilised doctor from the West Indies …

THE XENOPHOBIA – Closely related to the above, though not entirely identical to it. Etymologically speaking, the word *xenophobia* is derived from the Greek *xenos*, signifying both *guest* and *stranger*. Hence Basil's fear, not only of strangers, but also, and in particular, of *guests*.

THE MYTHOMANIA – Basil's inability to resort to the truth when trying to extricate himself from a difficult situation, usually of his own making. A notable exception to the rule occurs in The Psychiatrist, when Basil actually tries to tell the truth, only to find that Sybil refuses point-blank to believe him. The prime reason for Basil's problems in this episode is of a sexual nature. "He can't tell me anything about myself that I don't know already." In other words, the lucid interval in his obsession to speak the 'untruth and nothing but the untruth' is largely counterbalanced by his intense

---

3 It should be emphasised that the subdivision of Basil's mind into different categories does not indicate that his behaviour can at any time be regarded as the simple result of one or two identifiable mental disturbances. In reality his psyche represents a tumultuous totality of emotive actions and motifs, constantly changing both its inner and outer appearance, thus ultimately defying any attempt at definition. The following headings and their corresponding analyses should preferably be regarded as light flashes indicating possible access routes to the inner departments of the mysterious tower. Their sum total, however, does not equal the sinuous, swaying, tortuous tower itself.

uneasiness concerning anything having to do with – sex … Basil's compulsion to lie whenever possible, however, merits an investigation separate from that dealing with his lies of self-preservation.

THE MONEY OBSESSION – A vast field of contradictions. On one hand there is his penny-pinching (see for instance The Builders, or his complaint when having to open another bottle of Corton, "Right, but it'll cost me", in The Hotel Inspectors) and on the other hand his apparent munificence, his manifest indifference to money whenever he suspects nobility might be in the offing (A Touch of Class).

THE GAMBLING COMPULSION – Basil breaks out from to time to time, his obsession threatening ruin. For this reason he's always held under the most stringent surveillance by Sybil. Closely related to:

THE SYBILOPHOBIA – (also called by Basil, but only in moments when he is sure he's alone, *Sybilis*). In other words: Basil's morbid terror of his wife.

# THE CLASS PHOBIA

BRITAIN IS THE CRADLE of modern democracy. It is also, simultaneously, the home of Europe's most powerful and self-sufficient aristocracy *and* that of the absolute worst of the European mob. Now, imagine the fear which the latter demographic elements must necessarily inspire in someone who runs a typical cheaper hotel, while trying to attract a better clientele in order to exorcise what he sees as the stigma of his own social background.

Basil Fawlty is acutely and painfully aware of this dilemma, that he has in a sense manufactured for himself, and he tries, by any means open to him, to remain separate from the plebs. At the same time, a considerable part of him is still deeply imbued with references to the primitive side of modern life, to the practices of which he is no stranger. As a matter of fact, he was a good footballer in his youth and loved to watch the Saturday matches, just as he enjoyed going to the races, spending money he could ill afford lining the pockets of the bookies.

He never went straight home after these mild debaucheries. He stayed drinking at his local till time was called and the rougher elements fell out of the door to carry on their discussion on the pavement outside.

Still, though he loved the ambience of the pub, Basil was barely tolerant of his fellow-drinkers' vulgarity. He had no difficulty in convincing himself that this phase of his life was no more than an interlude, at once pleasurable and a touch degrading, to be forgotten and repudiated if he ever got to university, where he planned to devote his energies to scholarship, cricket and rowing.

But as we already know, his dreams of entry to university, with all its glittering prizes, eluded him. Instead, on that fateful evening, he met Sybil, who never bothered about her background and wisely refrained from wanting to seem finer or nobler than she was.

Her protests against Basil's gambling on horses and the pools reached their apogee when he notoriously began 'borrowing' from her – "just for a few hours dear", as he explained – only to find that the horse he put all her money on was an also-ran. One day she gave him an ultimatum: "It's either me or that horse." Basil chose the horse.

Sad to relate, it didn't win, so he now found himself in the humiliating position of having to prostrate himself before Sybil, of begging her forgiveness. She did forgive him, eventually, but only after relieving him once and for all of the cash-box key. It was the end of an era; he was never to get that key back. From that moment onwards, Sybil was mistress of the money; it was one of Basil's most painful defeats.

One day a certain Lord Melbury appears at hotel reception. Basil, who has suffered a surfeit of what he considers 'low-class' guests, sees in the newcomer yet another person of humble antecedents and therefore a suitable target for his particular brand of sarcasm.

When he finally realises that the new guest is in fact a real lord, his arrogance at once turns into the most embarrassing servility. And when his lordship, after having inveigled Basil into cashing a cheque, offers to have his collection of coins valued at a dinner party by that renowned numismatist, the Duke of Buckleigh, Basil's beside himself with self-importance, snobbery and dreams of wealth.

Although Lord Melbury makes little or no effort to conceal his kleptomania, ostentatiously pushing a hotel napkin up his sleeve in mid-conversation with Basil, for instance, the latter is still so much under the spell of the noble lord that he is influenced only by his own wishful thinking.

At first dumbfounded at the size of the sum demanded by Lord Melbury to cover his weekend expenses (£200 really was a lot of money in 1975 – compare for instance the price for a room with bath, £7.20, plus VAT, as quoted to Mrs. Richards in Communication Problems, 1979), Basil convinces himself how infinitely far removed from ordinary pecuniary concerns a lord must be, and breaks out into the sort of over-the-top reaction which establishes the crazy tone so typical of each of the ensuing eleven episodes.

However, the denouement of this first episode clearly indicates that Basil's veneration for members of the aristocracy in fact covers a deep and abiding resentment. For when he realises that he has been comprehensively conned, he loses all self-control in the presence of the newly arrived couple, Sir Richard and Lady Morris (incidentally the most hideous woman ever to set foot in Fawlty Towers). Basil does manage to recover the £200 from Lord Melbury, but, his rage unassuaged, is unable to hold back his contempt for Sir Richard and his lady, who hurry to their car and vanish.

Basil's relationship with elites of any kind is, to say the least, ambivalent, and is even more complicated by his tendency to confound nobility with education – a truly philistine misapprehension. In The Psychiatrist, Basil muses on Darwinian theory by contrasting the Neanderthal Mr. Johnson with the two doctors Abbott. He confides to Sybil: "Yes, nice to have that kind of person staying, isn't it? Professional class, educated, civilised." (He looks at Johnson): "We've got both ends of the evolutionary scale this week."

Whenever aristocratic or socially important figures are introduced to the series, however, they are mostly depicted as dull and unintelligent. There is the Gourmet Night's slightly handicapped Colonel Hall (he has a twitch), for instance, whose conversational range encompasses no more than the vagaries of the weather. But because of his exaggerated respect for anything to do with what he believes to be 'important people', Basil tries to maintain decorum, as he understands it, by avoiding introducing the Twitchens to the Halls for fear of drawing attention to the embarrassing similarity between the name of the former and the neurological affliction of the latter.

Sybil is of course well aware of her husband's somewhat anachronistic veneration of the aristocracy. In a passing reference to the alleged charm of cockney-speaking Mr. Johnson, in The Psychiatrist, she challenges Basil: "You seem to think that we girls should be aroused by people like Gladstone and Earl Haig and Baden Powell, don't you?" Basil's response is particularly revealing. "Well, at least they had a certain dignity. It's hard to imagine Earl Haig wandering round with his shirt open to the waist, covered with identity bracelets."

Whatever one may have to say about the British upper classes, one would have to admit that generally speaking they obey (or at least obeyed) precepts of decent behaviour, and comport themselves unexceptionably in public. This is a basic tenet of Basil's in matters concerning 'high' society, and it goes to show how little he actually expects from people – any kind of people.

In fact, one of his main aims in life is to keep everyone at a certain distance, and since it is a typical plebeian trait to hint at intimacy with people one scarcely knows (as both Sybil and Mr. Johnson do) Basil makes a virtue out of what he sees as an aristocratic creation of an unbridgeable gulf between the vulgar individual and the man of distinction – that is, himself.

# THE SEXUAL PHOBIA

A GREAT DEAL OF British humour is based on the idiosyncratic attitude of the 'decent' Englishman towards eroticism. Basil Fawlty is not only an example of this; he is the summation of classic British prudishness.

For non-British people the following may be crucial information. British boys and girls over several generations have had something of their view of the sexual world influenced by their visits to the pantomime, of which a recurrent feature is men dressing up and acting as women – generally old, comic women. The Monty Python universe is pervaded by this kind of transvestism. All the group's members used to dress up regularly in women's clothing. It suffices to recall the famous theme song, "I'm a lumberjack and I'm okay", to have tangible proof of their transsexual raptures.

Terry Jones (the incarnation of Brian's mother in *Life of Brian*) used to excel in female roles – in fact he hardly ever appeared out of them. Eric Idle had a great fondness for portraying gossipy ladies and venerable judges who revealed themselves as transvestites. Cleese himself appeared from time to time, and with considerable sadistic satisfaction, in grim female guises, such as Little Red Riding Hood with an axe in her hand.

Basil Fawlty, on the other hand, is the poor blighter who was never able to use laughter to lessen the weight of the terrible burden of repressed sexuality. To him, sexuality is a sinister reality whose frivolous aspects presage the decline of Western civilisation as he knows it. And that's why it is one of the sources of endless domestic conflict chez the Fawltys.

It is permissible to assume that by the time we get to know them, Basil and Sybil have developed what may euphemistically be termed 'marital problems'. We might just about envisage Sybil's enduring a Saturday night knee-trembler, in her flouncy nightie, in the dark, under cover, but the plaint, "Basil, not now. I have a terrible headache" is probably heard more and more frequently now.

Basil's advances are sometimes rejected, sometimes stoically borne. Either way, any reference during daylight hours to this shameful activity makes him extremely nervous and irritated.

Sybil would no doubt have liked things to be different (that is, she wishes there was some spark between them still) but she has stopped talking to Basil about it. (Audrey, by contrast, is privy to all these confidential matters.) A consequence of their childless – and on that account all the more cerebral – marriage, is an unavowed yearning on the part of both for love. Sybil is able at times to admit this to herself, but she can't always contain her acrimony whenever she thinks about what Basil doesn't or simply cannot give her.

Basil, who doesn't want to consider their floundering sexual intimacy a problem, refuses to realise that there may be a causal link between his own hysteria and Sybil's frigidity – and he would never openly recognise that he sometimes actually wishes that he were capable of being unfaithful.

However, we as onlookers should not consider this a sad state of affairs. Without these sexual frustrations, obviously, the entire rationale of Fawlty Towers would have collapsed.

There is substantial proof of this in that no fewer than three attempts have been made in the U.S.A. to adapt the idea of Fawlty Towers to the taste of U.S. television audiences. The first, called *Snaveley*, was produced during the summer of 1978 by Viacom and ABC, and never got past the pilot stage. Cleese himself, in an interview for the Los Angeles Times, suggested that the reasons for its failure was that "the producers feared it (the real Fawlty Towers) was too mean-spirited", and that there was "a noticeable attempt to reassure the audience that the people in the show were all right folks."

In 1983 the same companies again collaborated in an effort to bring forth a replica of Fawlty Towers. It was called *Amanda's by the Sea*, featuring a female character (played by Bea Arthur) in the main role. Here the Basil-type character was not merely relegated to the background, but omitted entirely! The series was planned to run in six parts, but only one episode was shot. It was a lamentable travesty of everything that Fawlty Towers stood for. Would you be able to imagine the hotel run by Sybil alone? It would just work smoothly, and where's the fun in that?

Finally, as recently as 1998, a project was launched by CBS, involving an interesting deal for John Cleese and Connie Booth. The series, named *Payne* (after the hotel owners, Royal and Constance Payne) went on air with an initial nine episodes. The show was apparently better conceived and executed than its predecessors, but lacked the sexual frustrations inherent in the original – Mrs. Payne having too much sex appeal to accurately replicate Sybil's dilemma, and Mr. Payne being far too liberal to be at all likely to accommodate the moral contortions which form such important constituents of Basil's problems.

This is at least what I have been able to discern from descriptions of and comments about that series (I have not myself seen any of the above-mentioned shows), and apparently even such a topic as Breeze's sexuality (Breeze being the allotrope of Polly) is discussible in Payne. It would have been strictly out of order for Sybil and Basil to venture on to such potentially hazardous ground.

The question thus arises: is Fawlty Towers in its original version at all accessible to American viewers? Strange as it may seem, its lack of a modern ethos (especially in relation to sex and drugs) does not prevent enlightened American viewers from drawing immense pleasure from it. From my own first-hand experience I can certify that the four video cassettes comprising the entire series were almost invariably unavailable from the video stores I frequented during a one-year stay in Los Angeles. Most of the people with a sense of humour I spoke to in Los Angeles knew exactly what the series was about, and they quite often had a few pertinent quotes up their sleeves to be used on the right occasion.

Rather than compare Fawlty Towers with any of its imitators, it would be more to the point, I think, to place its psychological core in relation to that of another, and this time very successful, American television show. Although *Married with Children* (featuring the shoe salesman Al Bundy, his busty, red-haired wife and two kids) has nothing in common with the former in most respects, there is one common factor – the secret horrors of a marriage that has become abhorrent but apparently indissoluble.

On a personal note, in the case of my own first and probably last marriage, I had the ambiguous privilege of watching myself gradually metamorphose into a perfect Basil-clone (almost needless to add that my wife simultaneously became more and more like the old dragon). I heard myself dropping deeply ironic remarks which were beyond my wife's comprehension ("It's called 'style', dear – you would never understand"). I heard her in turn constantly asking me to do this or not to do that, with the result that I became clumsy and irrational, misplacing things, falling off ladders, backing my car into others. In short, I was Basil. I could hear myself deliver lines which were veritable quotes from an imaginary and virtually endless Fawlty Towers; I observed myself turning into the captured male, hands and feet tied to the domestic totem pole, reduced to vindicate myself against my savage aggressor through verbal retaliation.

I dare say that any intelligent married man has a latent Basil germinating within himself. If he is lucky, the Basil within never receives the stimulus appropriate to his developing into a real monster, but it is upon this possibility that the series' uncanny projection and its almost irresistible attraction rests.

It is worthy of note that many (not all!) women who watch the series instinctively side with Sybil, and feel sorry for, and protective of, Manuel. To them Sybil is a quite normal and reasonable woman, and Manuel daft but harmless, and at least eager to please, whereas Basil inevitably gets everything monstrously wrong. On a superficial level there is some justification for this reading of the situation, but from a deeper perspective it's not only faulty, but also, surely, a sign of a petty and ungenerous way of observing reality. Above all, it's a non-humourous way of looking at it.

In the liberated republic of humour, Basil may be seen as a genius who for some reason has got stuck in a situation far below his real station. His powers of imagination, even if askew, are so vast that he simply must misinterpret the most commonplace, everyday events. His measureless exaggerations and inappropriate actions are the manifestations of superhuman creative and affective forces held captive by Lilliputians. His majestic intellect resembles the magnifying glass through which the flea appears an elephant. No wonder that nobody understands what he is talking about: his is a true prophetic voice crying in the wilderness.

He belongs in an altogether different world; his tragedy is that he doesn't have the minimal comfort or assurance of knowing it. He is a fallen angel, a Gnostic lost in material confusion. The conflict between his superior intelligence on the one hand, and his near-complete inability to cope with the material world on the other, is the primum mobile of the crazy, other, universe he unfurls before our eyes.

*Basil: Zoom! What was that? "That was your life, mate." That was quick, do I get another? "Sorry, mate, that's your lot."*

*Sybil: Basil.*

*Basil: Back to the world of dreams. Yes, dear?*

Only an enlightened mind perceives reality thus, and we mustn't forget that John Cleese, the mastermind behind this sudden illumination, was in 1978-79 working simultaneously on the production of the second set of Fawlty Towers and ex-Python Terry Gilliam's film production, *Life of Brian.* This film is entirely predicated on a non-orthodox conception of Christ. Along with mockery of revolutionary groups and their sectarianism, there is a Gnostic undertone to the film's message, namely, "See through the illusions of the world, judge for yourself and do not fall prey to moral fanaticism. Be a Jesus unto yourself."

To equate oneself with Jesus has always in the view of the established Christian churches been considered the most malignant of heresies. It is precisely this hubristic self-identification with Jesus that lies at the root of gnosticism, a doctrine much in vogue among enlightened people in the Mediterranean area during the first centuries of our era. By stressing the spiritual ubiquity of Christ at the expense of his historical aspect, the Gnostic doctrine acquired some resemblance to Buddhist teachings, where the Buddha is considered as being not so much a historical figure as a state of mind. (I make reference to this because Basil's lightning-quick reflection, "Back to the world of dreams" encapsulates references to

Gnostic as well as Hindu conceptions of this world as a veil of illusion.)[4]

To an enlightened Gnostic mind, sexuality represents an element of the obfuscation of true perception. Entangled in a web of constant illusion, while always claiming to be completely free from it, Basil is destined to have very serious problems. The sexual Freudian slip, therefore, is a constituent of many of Basil's spontaneously arising mishaps, notably in the two episodes, The Psychiatrist and The Wedding Party, where his sexual phobia is the dominant theme of the drama.

In The Psychiatrist – a truly sublime episode – we witness the superimposition of his obsession with social status onto his sexual paranoia, with the ensuing total eclipse of all his mental faculties.

As soon as the young and sexy Mr. Johnson appears on the scene, the tone is set. Sybil, making no effort to conceal her fascination, is intent on wounding Basil by way of his Achilles heel. She opens her campaign by dropping a suggestive remark to Mr. Johnson about the number of messages he has received during his brief absence from the hotel. We have at this juncture already been led to infer (by overhearing Sybil's side of a telephone conversation) that her closest friend, Audrey, has been physically attacked by her lover (presumably the infamous George) and is now, as a

---

4 It is well known that John Cleese – perhaps in particular during the years succeeding the Fawlty Towers era, in which he and his therapist Robert Skynner published two books dealing with some of the psychological problems facing modern man – took much interest both in traditional Buddhism and what might loosely be termed modern Christian mysticism, propounded by guru-like figures like Ouspensky and Gurdieff. Against the background of his general culture, as well as his academic training, Cleese was certainly, and from early on, also aware of the alternative interpretations of Christ that existed at the very inception of the Christian era, in order words, of gnosticism. I myself remember hearing Cleese say in an interview that he imagined Christ to be a person whom he would find very easy and natural to talk to, a striking individual, to be sure, but not so much by his apparent holiness, as by the sympathetic simplicity of manners.

consequence, suffering from a nosebleed. (Sybil, to herself: "I don't know why she stays with him.") Basil, having found the speaking clock engaged, though his wife is not talking to it, has withdrawn to the office. Upon Sybil's jolly remark to Johnson: "Oh well, you're only single once!" he interjects, sarcastically, and out of view: "Twice can be arranged!"

This hypothetical assumption (as far as Basil's own marriage goes) is the starting-point of a series of neurotic complications which become more convoluted with every effort of Basil's to mend fences. Sybil's forthright and unabashed remarks as to the attractiveness of Mr. Johnson force Basil to define what he means by masculine virtues.

Sex-appeal doesn't come into the question – Basil's ideal turns out to be the perfect English gentleman and aristocrat. Realising that not every man who qualifies as a gentleman in modern society can be nobly born, he benevolently extends the criterion to encompass education, dry wit and civilised behaviour in general.

Sybil, on the other hand, makes no secret of her wish to have a man who would, at least in bed, behave as a man and not a gentleman, and continues to rub salt into Basil's wound. Although Sybil is capable, superficially at least, of observing the conventions of polite society, she is never more than a step away from her own innate vulgarity (see, for instance, the opening scene of The Hotel Inspectors, where another of those uninhibited conversations with Audrey may be overheard by anyone, guest or staff, within earshot). If necessary, she will tell a lie and ratify it with a confident smile.

For example, in The Kipper and the Corpse, she tells Dr. Price, who would have liked some sausages for dinner (it is past 9:00 p.m.): "Oh, I'm afraid chef will have locked them away." As a matter of fact, this is one of the most automatic and recurrent lies one's likely to hear in the hotel and restaurant business.

Like Basil, Sybil sometimes displays a stunning lack of tact, as in the beginning of Gourmet Night, when she badly embarrasses André, as Basil is only too eager to point out. Her laugh can be a thing of dread, and she is not above obliging hapless guests to endure her soliloquies. One example of this occurs in the opening scene of Waldorf Salad, in which she obtusely intrudes on Mr. Libson's much-desired privacy. Subsequently, she reads and smokes next to the Hamiltons as they dine. In The Psychiatrist she rattles on interminably about her mother and her mother's "death force", totally oblivious of Johnson's complete lack of interest.

When speaking to Mr. Johnson she displays an infatuation with pagan symbols and superstitions which are in perfect harmony with the waiting room literature she so avidly reads in her leisure hours. As we already know, Sybil was working as a hairdresser when she first met Basil, in fact, the course she took in hairdressing was the only further education she ever had. She was taught her trade in the early 1960s, when the beehive and other heavily augmented hairstyles were all the rage, and Sybil remained faithful to this coiffure, even though it became quite out of fashion by the mid-1970s.

In her way Sybil is just as much an anachronism as Basil. The hippie movement passed her by without her even noticing. All her ideals were shaped by her petit-bourgeois environment, which goes some way to explaining why she now seems so much to regret the absence of all the fun she could have had in life, if only she'd known better. But then again, her lower-middle-class instincts are so strong that she will never be able to break free of their confines and pass beyond the narrow horizon of the *petite commerçante.*

Small money matters, clothes and interior decorating make up her world at home, conversations with Audrey and at the hairdresser's provide her with the gossip she needs for her intellectual fulfilment. And she's a golfer, too.

When she sees young Johnson, she thinks to herself how marvellous it must be to be a pagan, a hedonist, a free spirit. In The Anniversary she explicitly articulates her disappointment in this respect. "Fifteen years I've been with you," she says, "When I think of what I might have had." She's in much the same state of mind as she concocts a rather childish excuse to take a closer look at Johnson's hairy chest and tight leather trousers. Such obvious provocation naturally makes Basil disparage her intelligence all the more, as does her equating of sex appeal with Johnson's rather simian attributes – "Monkeys know how to enjoy themselves. That's what make them sexy, I suppose." The war between reason and instinct is fully engaged when the three doctors Abbott appear.

Basil is by now imitating a gorilla to prove that he is just as capable of having fun as the dreaded Johnson. On hearing Sybil's addressing the lady as "doctor" he leaps up on the reception counter. Being incapable of understanding that a woman can be academically educated, logic simply deserts him. The veneer of civilisation also begins to wear thin indeed, as he falls prey to his wildest fears. One of these is that some other person might prove able to discern the nature of his psychological dilemma, and, worse, to suggest some kind of treatment for it.

Like most men who have a marked tendency to rationalisation, Basil is utterly unaware of the real force of his instinctual urges. He represses them as best he can, burning so many bridges behind him that the only thing left for him to do is to continue moving forward, head-on towards inevitable catastrophe.

Once Basil has assimilated the fact that the gentleman newly arrived with his doctor-wife is a psychiatrist, he is almost paralysed with fear. Knowing next to nothing about either discipline, he confounds medical psychiatry with Freudian psychoanalysis. The folly of his rapidly mounting paranoia expresses itself in the conviction that a psychiatrist never rests from his perfidious activities, but instinctively looks for new subjects of study – or victims – wherever he can find them. When Sybil sees how truly afraid Basil is of being found out, she almost feels sorry for him. Basil, in his terror, can't or won't take this on board. And his worst fears are realised.

In a rare moment of tenderness, Sybil now tries to calm Basil down, realising that he is about to run amok. In her view their shared problem can be defined in simple and straightforward terms, and she wouldn't mind talking about it. "Now, if I had the money to go to a psychiatrist, he's just the sort I'd choose. I can't think of anything nicer than having a good old heart-to-heart. I'm sure they understand women" (pronounced 'wimin'), the unspoken corollary being that her husband doesn't, and never will.

The secret agenda underlying Sybil's display of admiration for Johnson comprises not only the arousal of Basil's jealousy, but also the arousal of Basil in general, in other words, to make him erotically interested in her again. Sybil does in her way love Basil, and even admires – if only intermittently – his 'sledge-hammer' wit. It has taken Basil years to educate her to the point where she is able to display a certain wit of her own. Mrs. Hamilton: "How long how you been married, Mrs. Fawlty?" Sybil: "Since 1485." (Waldorf Salad.)

Sybil's razor-sharp remarks ("She can kill a man at ten paces with one blow of her tongue," Basil tells O´Reilly in The Builders), is actually a defence mechanism she has developed to combat Basil's biting irony. Sybil used to be less judgemental towards people in general before she met Basil. He forced her into hardness and cynicism. But when Basil now shows signs of real vulnerability, not simply of confusion in general, she is stung by her conscience. All she wanted was to make Basil more aware of her needs as a woman. But alas, her attempt to put everything right between them comes too late: Basil is already on the brink of yet another mental breakdown.

From the moment he thinks he hears the Abbotts asking him

how often he and his wife perform the act of love, he gets sex on the brain. When his misgivings about Dr. Abbott have finally been allayed and the misunderstanding resolved, he is free to re-focus all his fear and hatred onto the odious Mr. Johnson – not, however, before greeting at reception a very attractive young Australian, Raylene Miles.

Sybil had her feelings under perfect control while she was flirting with Johnson, but Basil is both delighted and obviously invaded by a sense of shame as he finds his eyes reluctant to stray from Raylene's attractively filled cleavage. In the preceding kitchen scene, Cleese had developed a finger-and-hand language marvellously appropriate to Basil's neurosis. The verbal slips between private "parts" and "details" are accompanied by very nervous finger-movements on the part of Basil's left hand, which he keeps in the depths of his trouser pocket, giving the impression that he is playing with his genitalia down there.

Men often add to the more overt behaviour they adopt before attractive members of the opposite sex a secret sense of shame. This primarily expresses itself in unusual hand and arm movements – who has not in the presence of a sexy woman felt suddenly that he didn't know what to do with his hands?

Basil's hands begin to behave in a strange and defensive way when he has to explain to the ravishing Miss Miles where to put her signature. Considering the many 'involuntary' caresses he subsequently bestows on her, safety measures were necessary, albeit insufficient. Even if Basil had kept his hand out of the way of doing harm, he would still not have been able to keep his fingers away from the lady. That's the nature of his problem. Sybil, entering the scene at the moment when Basil has begun to take a putatively numismatic interest in the 'charm' dangling athwart her shapely bosom, is now, and as punishment for her earlier transgressions, overcome by genuine jealousy.

This is the crux of the episode. From this point onward we witness something unique: *Basil trying to speak the truth*. This is so unusual, so out of character, that Sybil finds it impossible to believe him. Knowing Basil to be a pathological liar who would make up a story even if he didn't have to, she simply refuses to give him the benefit of whatever doubt there might be. Her unbridled jealousy precipitates him into the abyss.

It must of course be understood that Sybil's jealousy alone would not be sufficient to give rise to so powerful a cataclysm. Basil is trapped by his utter inability to acknowledge the powerful physical attraction Miss Miles exerts on him. But since he is also unable to admit the existence of a correspondingly strong defence mechanism against arousal – the fear of punishment Sybil inspires in him – he feels compelled to transfer the problem to somebody else. The *deus ex machina* is Johnson, who happens to arrive at precisely the moment when Basil most desperately needs to shift the burden of his guilt.

The script does not quite convey the real action in this short but crucial scene. Both Basil and Sybil crouch down at this point to look for the order forms, so neither sees Johnson signal that the coast is clear for another pretty girl to pass upstairs unseen. The filmed version, however, clearly shows that Basil actually does see the girl. But it is not until he later hears Johnson utter his by-now infamous phrase, "Pretentious – *moi*?" that he makes the connection between the two events.

This crucial association in Basil's mind is preceded by the incredible scene in which, from inside the bathroom, he reaches his hand round for the light switch and makes contact instead with one of Miss Miles' breasts. At this very moment Sybil enters the room with a bag that Miss Miles has left behind at reception. Basil's predicament is getting minute-by-minute more and more desperate. Suddenly everything has begun to conspire against him in deadly earnest.

On his way back downstairs, still with the hope of making Sybil believe him, he hears a voice from Johnson's room, and realises that he has someone in there with him. Aha! The girl he just saw run up the stairs! Basil must seize this opportunity to put everything right again. In reviving his crusade against extra-marital sex, he now has an excellent pretext for not dealing with his own crisis. Winning back Sybil's confidence, maybe even her affection, will be a piece of cake once she has been made to understand that all he wants is to act in the best interest of Queen, country and English manners.

The moment has come for a favourite stand-by to come into play. This had been introduced in the third episode of the first series, The Wedding Party. ("Not married, is that it? Well, I can't give you a double room then. The Laws of England. Nothing to do with me.") In The Psychiatrist we witness a wonderful variation on this theme of bigotry and sexual repression.

To get back into Sybil's good books, and at the same time to get even with her, Basil needs proof that her favourite, Johnson, has acted immorally. Once this proof is forthcoming Sybil won't have any hold over him, and they'll be back to square one. 'It's either him or me,' Basil tells himself. Johnson has to go down.

Once the premise has been clearly stated the action proceeds with inexorable logic. The viewer is more or less obliged to take this point of departure for granted and to identify with Basil's rather bizarre attempt to get himself in the clear. In actual fact, his only trump card is that he has an obsolete Victorian ordinance supposedly on his side. Even though Sybil personally couldn't care less (as proven by her solution of the same problem evoked by Basil in The Wedding Party), she can't put things straight this time, simply because her jealousy won't allow her to find out what Basil is really up to.

Basil's insistence on his inalienable right to solve the problem single-handed makes this a 'winner-take-all' game. And he has no idea of how high the stakes will rise once the cards have been dealt.

First, he doesn't realise how cold-blooded his antagonist is. Just like a chess player who believes that he has his opponent helpless, Basil is sure that he's got his man stone-dead.

Once he's gained access to Johnson's room with the bottle of champagne, he doesn't have the courage to look into the bathroom, though he knows for sure that Johnson's little friend has to be in there. Instead he irrationally tries to collect evidence, lipstick on a cigarette stub, for instance. This proves a fatal mistake. A golden rule in chess is: "If you *can* attack, then you *must*." Add to this the confusion Manuel injects into the situation "I tell her (Mrs. Fawlty) you go to see girl in bedroom. You crazy about this girl, OK? So you go up to look at her, and Mrs. Fawlty, she go crazy", and we have all the essential ingredients of an emotional Molotov cocktail.

If Basil had had the patience to watch the door until it opened in the morning, he might still have been able to force a draw with his opponent – Johnson would have enjoyed his night of unhallowed bliss, admittedly, but Basil would have made his moral point and cleared himself before Sybil. But, alas, he is all too easily diverted.

The last act adapts masterfully to a different context the classic trick with three cups, under one of which an object is hidden. There are three doors and one Basil, who from his hiding-place in the hall cupboard has to guess when the one, behind which his quarry lurks, will open. In ordinary circumstances this would have required his undivided attention. Here he begins by mistaking the Abbotts and then Miss Miles for his prey.

With fateful precision he places not merely a fingerprint but a entire black handprint on that young lady's bosom. Realising that Sybil has made the inevitable connection between his black hand and its print on Miss Miles' chest, his mental faculties suffer a momentary, but total, short circuit. In an act of complete irrationality he leaps to her other breast and covers it with black as well. "Sorry, I got confused."

Under constant fire from Sybil, and still unable to contain his strong if unacknowledged attraction to Miss Miles, he becomes so confused that he leaves a breach in his plans fatally unguarded. He enters Miss Miles' room to apologise, thereby allowing Johnson just enough time to open the cage and let out his little friend.

Nonetheless, convinced of the absolute success of his plan, Basil allows himself the luxury of using physical force as well as verbal aggression against his demon-wife (as he sees her) in proving his innocence. The lines he delivers to the dumbfounded Sybil express the tremendous aggression and resentment he feels against his oppressor.

The time has come to settle the score. It is only here and at the end of The Anniversary that we witness Basil using a certain amount of physical force to dominate Sybil. (Even Sybil usually considers herself better off than poor Audrey, subject to George's violent mood swings.) Nowhere else in the series do we hear him speak his mind with such sincerity and eloquence as in the closing scene of The Psychiatrist. Basil is so convinced of his imminent victory that even his terror of Sybil is momentarily set aside. He feels absolutely fireproof, that he can get away with murder. And what murder! "I'm fed up with you, you rancorous coiffeured old sow. Why don't you syringe the doughnuts out of your ears and get some sense into that dormant organ you keep hidden in that rat's maze of yours?"

These are the words of a man sure of his aim and master of his destiny. "Mother Johnson, Mother Johnson," he carols. "Come out, come out wherever you are." A nice elderly lady appears smiling on the threshold.[5]

---

5 How she managed to get into her son's hotel room so quickly, and completely unnoticed, is problematic, unless we assume that she used the ladder left below the window by Basil the night before.

The defeat is total and irremediable. The fall from the heights of euphoria to utter despair does not stop short even of the womb. In an unsuccessful attempt to disappear, to crawl out of his own skin, he curls up in the classic foetal position. One moment he's Caesar at The Rubicon, the next a defenceless caterpillar on the floor, the very picture of an acute, pathological mania.

Another episode in which Basil's sexual phobia plays a major role is The Wedding Party. Flirty French Mrs. Peignoir takes a fancy to Basil, and makes no secret of it. The pivotal point of the drama is the intense embarrassment Basil experiences whenever he has to counter the lady's veiled, but less-than-totally discreet remarks. Hysteria announces itself in the first scene during the cocktail hour in the lounge. Sybil, giving vent to her characteristic laugh (the sound of a seal barking while being gunned down) is entertaining some rather vulgar male acquaintance at the bar.

Mrs. Peignoir approaches her prey, and Basil is moved to adopt what he imagines to be Gallic politeness. (His *enchanté* is not at all appropriate, being the response one uses when being formally introduced.)

*Basil:* (at his very best) *Ah, good evening, Mrs. Peignoir.*

*Mrs. Peignoir: Good evening. Thank you for your map, it was so useful. I had no idea how charming Torquay is.* (Sybil watches her for a moment, with a distinct lack of enthusiasm.)

*Basil: Enchanté. May I ask – did you find anything of interest?*

*Mrs. Peignoir: Mmm. A few pieces I liked very much, and one, oh!* (with flashing eyes) *I had to have it!*

In thus showing her passion, strong appetite and determination to acquire a coveted object, she instils in Basil a sense of foreboding, a feeling that he may well be next in line in her list of things desired. At once he's overcome by shame – and fear of Sybil's only too easily aroused jealousy.

In psychological terms the situation is very similar to the aforementioned scene in The Psychiatrist. To free himself from a sense of guilt (for the sin of adultery, even if only imagined) he's compelled to seek out some irreproachable moral cause in order to keep his conscience clear in relation to Sybil. (It is instructive to note that Sybil herself never feels guilt about her little flirtations – for some reason women have much less sense of responsibility or shame in matters of this kind than men.)

As in The Psychiatrist, the moral cause required by Basil offers itself. The first to suffer its consequences are Alan and Jean, the young couple arriving on the eve of the wedding party. Finding that they aren't married, Basil of course refuses to give them a room with a double bed. It takes Sybil to sort things out and do the natural thing.

Any male and married person not suffering from excessive sexual repression would by this point have cleared his conscience in relation to his partner. But Basil hasn't even started yet. The intensification of his erotic fantasies, his emotional disorder and his general propensity for messing things up range from his inferring from Alan's question if the chemist's was still open that he needs to buy condoms and batteries for his girlfriend's vibrator, to the unforgettable, "I'm so sorry. I made a mistake."

Still, even after he has seen the light and somehow disentangled himself from the web of his delusions, he's unable to shake off the uneasy feeling Mrs. Peignoir inspires in him – especially during that warm night when Sybil has left the hotel to tend the ever-ailing Audrey. Here Mrs. Peignoir uses the stuck bedroom window as a convenient pretext to inform Basil that, "I shall sleep *au naturel* tonight – only it's not so much fun on your own."

Convinced that it must be Mrs. Peignoir who is knocking at his bedroom door ("I won't try and sit on you again!") in the middle of the night, he invents a scenario in which his wife is supposed to have come back – she is in the bathroom, perilously close to over-hearing their daring conversation.

*Basil: Look, you'll meet somebody else sooner or later.*

*Sybil: Let me in!*

*Basil: Shut up, will you, you silly great tart. Go away! My wife will hear us!*

*Sybil: This is your wife!*

(Suddenly he realises the situation. He has exactly three seconds to come up with an explanation. He opens the door and faces Sybil.)

*Basil: Oh, what a terrible dream!*

Luckily for him Sybil's mind is elsewhere. The supposed burglar is Manuel waking up from his alcohol-induced coma in the laundry basket.

In Waldorf Salad we see yet another instance in which Basil's sexual neuroses gain the upper hand. One might imagine that it would make no difference to him whether Terry's negotiated ex-tra money was to be spent on karate classes or on entertaining a blonde Finnish girl. But to Basil this makes all the difference in the world. The very thought that Terry managed to wring some extra money out of him, money destined to be spent on pleasures of a carnal nature, is not to be borne. He would be guilty of an abominable crime of omission if he allowed Terry to get away with this.

Although it would be more plausible for a hotel owner simply to use a moral argument in salving his conscience while at the same time making an extra buck, Basil's indignation is real. In other words, his aim is not primarily to make money, but morally to punish Terry for envisaging pleasures that are forbidden fruit, and, to Basil, anathema.

Mr. Hamilton, being an American and not accustomed to Basil's peculiarly English vision, later takes it for granted that Basil dismissed Terry so that he could keep the money for himself. He would have been astonished to learn that Basil's behaviour was in fact dictated by a very real moral indignation, and not by greed pure and simple. In this respect Basil was absolutely right when later informing Mr. Hamilton that "there are things far more important to us British than money" – namely, to suppress everything having to do with you know what …

# THE RACIAL PHOBIA

IT IS AXIOMATIC IN Basil's mind that God, if not altogether perfect, pretty well qualifies to be an Englishman. Nothing in his experience has ever suggested that English is not synonymous with civilisation – "Thank God we English can laugh at each other, eh?" Neither would it occur to him to question the intrinsic value of a civilisation that gave to the world free trade, democratic institutions and tea with buttered scones.

In Basil's mind it follows that other nations are barbarians to a higher or lower degree. Ireland and Scotland are the spoiled and ungrateful children of Britannia. Their claims to independence are ridiculous and almost incomprehensible considering that they owe everything to England and have nothing to offer in return other than whisky, Guinness, ceilidh music and kilts. Inevitably to Basil's way of thinking, therefore is, that the worst builder in England – O'Reilly – should be Irish.

The rest of Europe, with the exception of Germany, is just peculiar. The French have a strange language which they articulate through their noses. Their manners are licentious, and lascivious too – "Try to control yourself. Where do you think you are – Paris?" (Basil addressing the presumed Mrs. Peignoir on the other side of his bedroom door in The Wedding Party). The Spanish are all brothers of Manuel and consequently useless idiots –

"God knows how they ever got an Armada together." Americans are vulgar, ignorant, greedy, aggressive, loud and bragging (Waldorf Salad). The Greeks are probably all homosexuals (like the chef Kurt in Gourmet Night). And the Germans are unreconstructed Nazis – every last one of them – "Bad eggs." Basil has never regarded Polly's ambition to brush up her foreign languages as anything but a waste of time. If Germans don't understand English, well, that's their problem.

The truth is of course that Basil, profoundly uninterested in other nations and their peoples, finds it humiliating not to be able to dominate the situations in which he comes into contact with them. The prospect of having to listen and learn fills him with vague feelings of disgust. Polly, belonging to a species of a more gentle kind, does not attach the same importance to verbal domination over others.

But as far as Basil is concerned, even English people are foreigners of a kind inasmuch as they are guests (see also next chapter). Anyone making demands on Basil's time and attention is by definition a nuisance and an intruder, a member of an inferior race, most conveniently described as *riff-raff*.

Basil's character derives from an actual encounter with a Torquay hotel-owner (see Chapter 6), who must have been the worst-suited person imaginable to this metier – and Basil's character remains in many ways true to that of his prototype. However, even if Basil is at heart uninterested in attending to the needs of his guests, he still sometimes tries to accommodate foreign visitors, and in the case of Mrs. Peignoir even beyond the call of duty. But Mrs. Peignoir is at least French, and French phrases in Basil's mouth always indicate that he is trying to be polite, even charming. When it comes to Germans it is impossible for him to restrain his real affective impulses.

Racism comes quite naturally to Basil. I can imagine that his spiritual father, John Cleese, at some early stage even played with the idea of characterising Manuel as an Indian or a Pakistani. Circumstantial evidence in support of this association can be found in Basil the Rat, when Basil tries to explain to Manuel that two pigeons have to be removed from the water tank (Basil: "Not pigs, pigeons – like your English!") This is a reference to *pidgin*, a word which, although originally only denoting the English vernacular in places such as West Africa, and Papua New Guinea, is nevertheless commonly understood as the English spoken by indigenous elements of the Indian subcontinent.

Another piece of evidence innocently positing Manuel's Indian origins can be gathered from a dining-room scene in The Kipper and the Corpse.

*Manuel: He bite me!*

*Mrs. Chase: You frightened him* (her lap dog).

*Manuel: Qué?*

*Mrs. Chase: You make sudden movements like that, of course he's going to bite. Don't you have dogs in Calcutta?*

It would in a sense have made Manuel socially more plausible, had he been Indian. But it would also have entangled the creators of the comedy in an act of political provocation which may have subtracted rather than added to the universality of the concept. In addition, many jokes based on verbal misunderstanding would have been much weaker, if not completely meaningless, with a Hindi-speaking waiter – an essential feature of the show is in fact Basil's conviction that he knows how to speak Spanish, whereas Manuel doesn't! ("I learnt classical Spanish, not the strange dialect he seems to have picked up" (A Touch of Class). Nevertheless, even Basil at one point lets out a sigh of despair over Manuel with a subtle allusion to India: "Oh, Buddha" (The Germans).

Conversely, the invention of a good-hearted but half-witted European character who simply can't learn English was a stroke of genius insofar as it still permits Basil to give free rein to his sense of racial, social and intellectual superiority. In the case of Manuel, the problem evoked in Kipling's and colonial Britain's notion of The White Man's Burden is brought back to life. How does one communicate with a savage? Or, rather: how does one educate him so that he can both understand an order and carry it out correctly?

Apart from these obvious racial distinctions, the Spanish connotation also had the advantage of offering a literary archetype to the subliminal perception of the viewer. Already in terms of their physical statures, Basil and Manuel correspond perfectly to the famous couple in Cervantes' novel: the gallant, lankily tall picaro Don Quixote, famously attacking the wind-mills for the sake of winning nearer to his ever illusive Dulcinea, and his amazed, bewildered, simple minded, conspicuously short yet loyal squire Sancho Panza. The parallel is actually so obvious that it is easily overlooked. It is likewise obvious that it doesn't hold good in all respects, quite especially in this, that the great historical couple have a relationship based on the reassuring fact that both master and servant speak Spanish.

It doesn't take long to realise that Basil primarily uses Manuel as a surrogate whenever he'd rather smack his wife (or someone else, for that matter). By virtue of his poor English and modest intelligence, Manuel is the perfect scapegoat. Basil isn't quite sure where to place him on the evolutionary scale. Defining him as the missing link would conveniently place him somewhere mid-way between an ape and Dr. Livingstone. To judge from the very first episode, A

Touch of Class, Sybil actually puts him at an even lower stage of evolution. It was she who provided Basil with one of his favourite outbursts "It'd be quicker to train a monkey."

A variation on the theme of Manuel's evolutionary status can be found in Basil the Rat. Sybil: (speaking to Basil about Manuel's hamster) "Perhaps it would be simplest to have him put to S-L-E-E-P." Basil: "Who, him or the rat? We might get a discount if we had 'em both done."[6]

To the Major, Manuel might just as well be a poor kid from Bangladesh. The question is, does the Major actually see him as one? While leading monkey-walking Manuel away to show him how to get to the dining room via the back door of the kitchen, he is searching his memory in vain to recall what the staff used to call him (The Builders).

Speaking of apes and missing links, it is worth noticing that Basil in general favours a Darwinian, that is, a biological, view of society. His preoccupation with the idea that some people are more monkey-like than others extends, as we have seen, to include Mr. Johnson in The Psychiatrist, as well as Mr. Brown, alias Danny (the disguised cockney-speaking police agent in A Touch of Class). Although no explicit reference to the simian behaviour of the latter is made, we may readily imagine what Basil thinks. He is perfectly capable of being explicit, on the other hand. We remember his telling Manuel in The Builders to tell "man with beard"(Murphy), that "You are a hideous orang-utang." Basil (over the phone) says, "Well done, Manuel. Thank you very much."

---

6 For evolutionary reference, see also Sybil's not-so-favourable opinion of Irish cock-up-artist O'Reilly in The Builders. Sybil: "Not brilliant? He belongs in a zoo!" Another instance is Basil's comment to Manuel: "I'm going to sell you to a vivisectionist." (Communication Problems).

Similarily, Mr. Johnson in The Psychiatrist is at one point referred to as "the bravest orang-outang" in Britain.

Further proof of Basil's evolutionary preoccupation can be found right at the opening of Basil the Rat. Sybil has complained that he always has a reason against her meeting someone – "any other members of the human race," in fact. Almost inaudible to television viewers but clearly indicated in the script, Basil murmurs, "Yes, well, I wouldn't call the Sherrins members of the human race, dear."

Ideologically speaking, post-war social Darwinism appears in a variety of guises. Freed from its connection with eugenics and Nazism, it has come to be identified as one of the driving forces and principles of the free market. But Basil is far from seeing the social success of the simple money-maker as an example of the survival of the fittest. In his view one should be born to money. This, as he understands it, is the birthright of the English gentry. Basil, decidedly right-wing, perhaps a Thatcherite, has modernised his romantic affinity with lords and manors to encompass an ongoing struggle between any individual with aristocratic aspirations (himself) and "the much too many" (almost everybody else).

When in Waldorf Salad the snare begins to tighten around him, he is at first unable to realise the precariousness of his situation. In order to subdue mounting dissatisfaction with the service – once it has been brought to general attention by Mr. Hamilton – he tries to foist on his native guests a lot of sentimental rubbish, citing the nobility and idealism of the British soul. Handing over the money he earlier received from Mr. Hamilton to make the chef stay, he says, "I know how important it (money) is to you Americans. But you must remember that here in Britain there are things that we value more, things that perhaps in America you have rather forgotten, but that are, here in Britain far, far more important."

*Mr. Johnstone: I'm not satisfied ...*

When Basil sees that the dreaded guests have completely surrounded him and that his back is to the wall, he attempts a single-
leap solution.

> *Basil: Let me tell you something* (his eyes gleam dangerously).
> *This is exactly how Nazi Germany started. A lot of lay abouts with*
> *nothing better to do than to cause trouble!*

Now, if that is not playing for sky-high stakes I don't know what
is![7]

Another peculiar instance of Basil's 'racism' is his readiness to assume that the Major's latest pink elephant is in fact a German one
(Basil the Rat). From the corner of his eye, and at first unwilling
to believe what he's seeing, Basil observes the Major, shotgun in
hand, proceed to the bar. When the Major explains that he has
seen some vermin on the premises, Basil, without a second's
hesitation, misinterprets this to mean that the Major thought he
saw a German sitting on the table. The ensuing dialogue is worth
quoting in its entirety.

> *Basil: No Germans staying this week, Major. May I have the gun?*

---

7 It is noteworthy that the Ladies remain loyal to him in all circumstances, and of particular interest in this respect is the Major's exclamation in response to Mr. Johnstone's allega-
tion that "I think this is probably the worst hotel we've ever stayed in." The Major: "No, I
won't have that. There is a place in Eastbourne ..." In the published script – which claims
to be the complete and unexpurgated text of Fawlty Towers – this line is simply missing, de-
priving the reader of the pleasure of freely associating the Eastbourne hotel with the one in
Torquay where John Cleese and Connie Booth originally became acquainted with the Basil
prototype.

*The Major: Going to shoot him, Fawlty.*

*Basil: Yes, Major.*

*The Major: Mmm?*

*Basil: Not – not legal, actually, any more – murder …*

*The Major:* (in obvious astonishment) *But they are animals, Fawlty!*

*Basil:* (understanding and surprisingly lenient) *Oh, yes, yes. Still, forgive and forget, eh, Major?* (he takes the gun).

*The Major: Forgive 'em?*

*Basil: Well, pretend we do.*

*The Major: But they spread disease, Fawlty – he was sitting there on that table, eating the nuts if you please.*

*Basil:* (to himself) *He's really gone this time.*

In other words, Basil sees nothing directly appalling in what he believes to be the Major's instinctive reaction upon finding a German in the bar. The oddity is that there are no German guests present in the hotel, and that the Major's impression therefore must be interpreted as a delusion caused by a combination of alcohol and senile dementia in general. When the situation is finally cleared up, the fact that the hamster is loose is accepted with the same insouciance as the German on the table.

The Major: *About that size. That with the tail.*

Basil: *What did you say it was?*

The Major: *Vermin … a dirty rat!*

In the episode that does feature Germans, Basil doesn't really comport himself very well before his foreign guests. There are extenuating circumstances, however. Previously, having suffered the blow on the head from Manuel's frying pan, Basil had almost gone through the roof when unexpectedly meeting the coloured doctor who has come to treat Sybil's ingrowing toenail. To be black *and* a medical doctor is a contradiction in terms in Basil's universe. Even when he has overcome the first shock, he is still unable to rid himself of the suspicion that Dr. Finn is in reality a voodoo practising medicine man from the West Indies. He even pretends to fall asleep, as if under a spell, to the mystical head rotations Dr. Finn performs on him to keep him in bed. In this way Basil counters superstition with superstition: he believes he has outsmarted both *Unkulunkulu* and Sybil.

The episode The Germans consists of three distinctly separate actions. First, there is the hilarious farewell scene at the hospital ("Oh, no. No dogs allowed here"). Secondly, the fire drill, where once again, a big woman of somewhat mixed genetic background incarnates the kind of inquisitiveness which Basil invariably finds repulsive. Thirdly, there is the actual arrival of the Germans, presaging Basil's final breakdown. His Hitler impression at the end has a tendency to stay longest in the memory. It is however an obvious loan from the Monty Python sketch The Department of Silly Walks. Otherwise careful to avoid associating Fawlty Towers with typical Python gags, Cleese here succumbed to temptation. The big audience will always love him for it, but for the connoisseur this last scene has an *arrière goût* of playing to the gallery, which somewhat eclipses the brilliance of both acting and script in the previous scenes.

The important factor binding these three scenes together is actually the moose head, the one responsible for snagging Sybil's cardigans and, ultimately, for Basil's downfall. "It will lend the lobby a certain ambience, Sybil. It has a touch of style about it." But Basil will once again – when animals, Germans and generally brutish guests conspire to bring him down – live to regret his attempt to turn his modest hotel into a more up-market residence.

As a final, charming, reminder of the racial prejudice permeating the episode, I should cite both Manuel's, "Hello, I am English" from within the moose head, and the Major's assumption that the speaking moose surely must be of Japanese origin.

*Basil:* (bewildered) *Canadian, I think, Major.*

*The Major:* (candidly) *I didn't know the Canadians were as clever as that.*

It is symbolic that it was during the shooting of The Germans that Manuel's suffering as the underdog paradoxically became economically profitable to the actor playing the role. It is almost as if he had been granted some compensation for injuries contracted during wartime persecution, then, at this point we should remind ourselves that Andrew Sachs, like Charlie Chaplin, the Marx Brothers, Woody Allen, Lenny Bruce, Jerry Seinfeld, and many other first-class comedians, is of course Jewish.

# THE XENOPHOBIA

WE CONCLUDE FROM THE previous chapter that Basil is not very fond of strangers in general. We remember that the word *xenophobia* – irrational fear of strangers – derives from the Greek word *xenos*, signifying both stranger and guest. Imagine then Basil's frustration when suddenly a stranger announces himself as the unavoidable and very, very demanding guest ...

In addition to making outrageous demands ("Do you hire television sets!") Mr. Hutchison, the spoon salesman in The Hotel Inspectors, affects a convoluted English and a lordly, yet excessively pedantic manner which betrays him as a small man of modest background trying to be more important than he actually is. Basil, extremely sensitive to the nuances of class migration, wants to prick the balloon of Mr. Hutchison's pretensions right away.

> *Basil: It is not possible to reserve the BBC 2 channel from the commencement of this televisional feast until the moment of the termination of its ending. Thank you so much.*

> *Hutchison: Well, in that case, may I suggest you introduce such a scheme.*

> *Basil: No.*

*Hutchison: I'd just like to tell you that I have a wide experience of hotels and many of those of my acquaintance have had the foresight to introduce this facility for the benefit of their guests.*

*Basil: (unimpressed) Oh, I see, you have had a wide experience of hotels, have you?*

*Hutchison: Yes, in my professional activities I am in constant contact with them.*

The scene is set. Basil, seeing a possible link between the odious Hutchison and the likely presence of a hotel inspector in town, is obliged to make a 180° turn. At once his behaviour changes. He senses the sword of Damocles hanging over him. He must succeed with the impossible: to be nice, polite, obliging, even amiable, to the most irritating, inquisitive know-it-all he has ever had in his hotel. In normal circumstances, Basil would at this point already have finished Hutchison off by suggesting he move to a hotel with private television in the bathroom, a fridge full of ginger beer, medically sterilised use-and-throw telephones and a folding ping-pong table in the wardrobe.

But now certain that this is the man he must convince of the hotel's impeccable service and facilities, he makes use of the real gentleman, Mr. Walt, as a butt for his sarcasm and rudeness. Needless to add, of course Manuel, as usual, gets his daily dose of corrective therapy.

Bernard Cribbins, who plays the part of Mr. Hutchison, is one of Britain's finest comedians. His and Cleese's performances in The Hotel Inspectors complement each other as in a perfect piece of chamber music. Two virtuosi in the realm of humour here meet and play together. The result is stunning. We can imagine that they both enjoyed playing opposite someone of comparable stature.

There is special glee in Hutchison's twinkling eye when he responds to Basil's initial, "Are you all right?" with, "Oh, yes, I find the air here most invigorating." A secret sign, as it were, signifying: here we go! The crescendo is masterfully orchestrated, from the moment when Hutchison at the reception desk waves his finger obnoxiously to obtain Basil's attention, until the moment he falls unconscious into the cheese salad.

Both Basil and Hutchison are peculiarly immune to any kind of criticism – the scenario and script here give Basil the chance to demonstrate the depth of his indifference toward guests whose social status has failed to impress him, or who have proved incapable of responding to any of his needs. During Basil's honeymoon-period with Hutchison, Mr. Walt is badly treated by Basil, who has become virtually deaf and blind to everybody else except the agent from the hotel guide.[8] In a series of cruel misunderstandings, Basil is finally brought to confess, although he of course doesn't actually put it into words, that the hotel they run is all about appearances. Basil (now mistaking Walt for the hotel inspector): "Oh please, it's taken us twelve years to build this place up. If you put this in the book we're finished." As soon as it becomes clear to Basil that Mr. Walt sells outboard motors, his revenge on Hutchison is utterly studied and humiliating.

Although the short and sturdy Mr. Hutchison presents all his pe-

---

[8] Mr. Walt is incarnated by James Cossins, who in his career as a film actor also appeared as Q's assistant in the James Bond film, *The Man with the Golden Gun*. I find this an extraordinary coincidence since John Cleese recently has been appointed as the new Q (Or is it R? Anyway, it is a commitment for life!) in the Bond films. Maybe Basil, in spite of the catastrophe, really impressed Mr. Walt to the point that the latter, more than twenty years later, recommended him as successor to Q, expert on explosives and other murderous devices in Her Majesty's Secret Service. If this is true, he couldn't have made a more excellent choice. If it was down to me, I'd make Basil head of all the weapons laboratories in the world. If nothing else, that would put an end to them!

dantic observations as Napoleonic decrees, and although he himself, like his military model, ultimately goes down, he is in all his dedicated seriousness and will to ameliorate the services, a character with whom I personally can easily identify. I do not know how many times I have found myself in Hutchison's position: demanding beverages to be replaced because they were not cold, or simply not good enough, sending back hot dishes because they were cold, questioning the preparation at various stages ("food handling routines suspect!"), commenting upon the ingredients ("might I suggest that in future you avail yourself of sufficient quantities of the fresh article"- I love that one!), commenting on what the chef should and shouldn't do, making a fuss about the disproportion between stingy portions, small drinks and high prices. If provoked by inadequate services, I am prepared to go straight into the kitchen and make sure things are finally made the way I want them. In short, I am at times Hutchison. It would even occur to me to wipe the earpiece of the telephone because it really was greasy. And I do have a wide experience of hotels, bars and restaurants, then in my professional activities I'm in constant contact with them (study Hutchison's half-shut and ominously gleaming eye here).

What makes Hutchison so exceptional is his unusual persistence. Confronted with Basil, most people, even I, would sooner or later – and sooner rather than later – give up. Hutchison doesn't. "I want it (the diagram of the optimum route to the Post Office from Queen's Square) all the same!"

By virtue of his unusual stubbornness, Hutchison is Basil's equal, actually the only character throughout the entire series who is. He is also, to our knowledge, the only guest ever to be manhandled by Basil, and the only guest who in return physically attacks him. One understands that the complicity between them is of a rare and intimate kind. It takes one to know one …

But if Hutchison is Basil's equal, the latter really meets his match in Mrs. Richards (Communication Problems). In this episode we have the fresh pleasure of finding Basil's reactions rather understandable, not to say 'normal'. The reason why Basil here seems reduced to normal human proportions is simply that he is up against the Mike Tyson of heavyweight hotel guests. It is easy to understand Basil's problem in relation to Mrs. Richards, considering that nobody else, and that includes Sybil, finds a way to communicate with her. The dialogue between Basil and Mrs. Richards in her hotel room (Manuel in attendance) is one of the many Fawlty Towers highlights.

*Mrs. Richards: When I pay for a view I expect something more interesting than that.*

*Basil: That is Torquay, madam.*

*Mrs. Richards: Well, it's not good enough.*

*Basil: Well, may I ask what you were hoping to see out of a Torquay hotel bedroom window? Sydney Opera House, perhaps? The Hanging Gardens of Babylon? Herds of wildebeest sweeping majestically …*

This time we would rather have liked to witness success for Basil. Even though we know that every episode is a tragedy giving rise to tremendous, superhuman suffering on Basil's part, we still think this one might after all end on a happy note. But of course it doesn't. In the last round Mrs. Richards knocks Basil out. He had staked every penny on the most momentous gamble of his life, namely on himself. But the only piece of pure luck that has blessed Basil's long and dolorous path over the last fifteen years, is snuffed out like a candle in the wind. He simply can't win. And Manuel will solemnly keep the secret until the end of his days – "I know nothing!"

We remember that it is in Communication Problems that Basil interprets his suffering in Gnostic terms – "What was that, that was your life"... etc. Thus, he acknowledges the existence of something beyond this world, where nevertheless he must continue to live out his life. And to live in this world – the world *sub luna*, as medieval cosmogony describes the lowest and most rudimentary plane of existence – has for Basil above all the meaning of being watched over by a dragon that never sleeps and consequently can only be fooled by devices so cunning that they would make the tricks of Ulysses seem mere trifles in comparison. Here, for once, Basil thought he had outsmarted the cruel, ever watchful eye of his oppressor. Here, clearly, he saw escape from tyranny in the offing. Here, at last, he believed that he could save his life and begin to hope for future moments of true joy and excitement. Alas, all the other evils were already out of Pandora's box when hope was captured inside it. Brutally Basil is brought to face the immutable truth: there might be hope but there is no mercy.

Never have the notions of *guest*, *stranger*, and *enemy* been more confusedly and fatally associated in Basil's mind than in The Hotel Inspectors and Communication Problems. But of all Basil's defeats at the hands of his enemies, the one inflicted by Mrs. Richards was perhaps the most severe, because it shows, not only that Sybil is against him (he's used to coping with that), but also that the gods themselves have withdrawn all favour from him.

There is no reason to deplore his fate excessively, however. In other instances his behaviour to hotel guests is appalling, discourteous and insulting, to say the least. The worst example of his arrogance and abuse of guests may possibly be found in Waldorf Salad. Mr. Johnstone has irritated Basil by showing himself his equal in sarcasm. Commenting on the inedible prawns, he has suggested that they be deducted from the bill. But Basil, observing that Mrs. Johnstone has already eaten half of hers, won't give way. Whereupon Mr. Johnstone comments: "Well, deduct half now, and if my wife brings the other half up during the night, we'll claim the balance in the morning. And now we'd like our lamb, please."

That is a devastating riposte which would leave any ordinary hotelier speechless – even Basil is temporarily silenced. But in his heart hatred is stirring, awaiting the moment when vengeance will be exacted. Instead of giving the Johnstones their main courses right away, he takes the plates with him to the lobby as Sybil, busy with something else as always, has told him that there is a new guest at the reception.

This is Mrs. Hamilton, wearing an expensive fur coat. Basil is somewhat impressed by her. Mr. Johnstone has followed him out into the lobby and asks for the plates. They are handed over to him with a *"bon appétit"* followed by an onomatopoeic farting sound. Just imagine being thus treated as a paying guest in a hotel – and we may safely assume that this utter rudeness is only the tip of the iceberg! It begs the question how Fawlty Towers after twelve years of insults and non-existent service on the part of its proprietor, still manages to attract any clientele at all.[9]

Finally, to dot the i's and cross the t's, Basil not only loathes and abuses hotel guests, but even such guests and visitors as most other people would refer to as their friends. For example, the need to keep up appearances at all costs and never admit that he and Sybil

---

9 Human nature is indeed strange. I know of a restaurant in Stockholm called Svedala, where the principal attraction is its owner, who, on the slightest provocation, will not hesitate to correct the manners of his guests, teach them how to handle a knife and fork, etc. The restaurant is always full, and you have to reserve weeks in advance to get a table there.

have marital problems, turns the friends invited to The (wedding) Anniversary into potential enemies. It is actually only in this episode that we encounter any friends of the Fawltys. We even meet Audrey in her only public appearance, consoling Sybil in the car – "I guess I shouldn't be so thin-skinned about it. I'm just cursed with a sensitive nature" (preliminary confession to Polly about Basil's fatal negligence). Whereupon Basil's practical joke quickly becomes a nightmare.[10]

While Basil chases after her and Audrey in the car to disclose the joke and bring Sybil back, Roger and his wife arrive in their car. It does not occur to Basil to ask Roger to go after Sybil, although a quick explanation would almost certainly have sent his friend hotfoot after her. Basil obviously doesn't trust Roger's discretion and instead prefers to remain in his own deeply solitary universe, in which he is god and creator. In other words: Dispense with previous scenario; substitute completely new plot. Roger and his wife consequently find the wedding anniversary celebrating Basil on the driveway leading up to the Towers, pretending to even out a bump in the road.

With Sybil absent, Basil, unsurprisingly, treats his friends rather as he does his guests. Roger is the only one with any inkling of the spectacular fraud in the making. But his attempts to establish some intimacy with Basil by making puns ("Syb-ill", "Bas-ill", "Manu-well", etc.) are uncompromisingly rejected as Basil refuses to un-

---

10  The fact that Audrey here appears as the consoling angel, unaware of Basil's plans for the evening, clearly indicates that Basil hasn't invited her to the surprise party commemorating his and Sybil's fifteen years of marital bliss. Knowing that she really is Sybil's closest friend he has made sure that she will remain far from the scene of action on this occasion. So, even if Basil had been able to stop Sybil from going away, she would have had an excellent occasion for lashing out at him again. Sybil: "Why didn't you invite Audrey?" Basil: "But then I would have had to invite George as well, and you wouldn't have liked that, would you?" Etc.

derstand. However, the underlying cause of his indifference vis-a-vis Roger is not simply callousness and egotism, but his inability to admit that he is lying, and his compulsion to cover up one lie with another, and so on till the house of cards, as if ordered by divine vengeance, comes tumbling down.

Which brings us to the next heading.

# THE MYTHOMANIA

THE FOUNDATION OF THE comedy of life is the human experience that life itself is but a dream. What dream and comedy have in common is that they both draw upon the sources of the unconscious. Sigmund Freud was aware of the connection and devoted an essay to the problem, *The Joke and its Relation to the Unconscious*. His conclusion was that the joke represents a disarmed threat to the ego. An event that would arouse fear in one person is deactivated by being presented as happening to someone else. All laughter is at bottom laughter at another's expense. It can't be otherwise. The individual personifying the victim is the comic figure per se. Basil Fawlty, constantly exposed to all his worst fears, unable to arm himself against the unforeseeable, is condemned to live his life encapsulated in an eternal now. As such he becomes the slave of the unpredictable, and our hero.

In saying this, I don't mean that we spectators are in a better situation than Basil's. The fleeting sensation of an unavoidable present is the essence of our reality too. Most of us are able to foresee certain consequences of our actions, based on experience, but in this sense Basil has no past and no future. All experience is obliterated in the face of a present threat to his person. Being unable to see any further into the future than the end of his nose, he rushes headlong into danger as if it doesn't exist, only to invent endless excuses for not having had the courage finally to face up to it (I think I *may* have acted that way myself on occasion …).

When, exceptionally, his own desire happens to coincide with factual circumstances, a generally accepted reality, or even with the truth, Basil uses this to gain an advantage – which means that all Basil's statements, regardless of whether they are true or false, are ruthlessly subjective. His interactions with others are based on the premise that other beings – and even inanimate objects – are actively harmful to his own purposes. For him to live is to get away from (or with) something – in most instances the burden of other people and the tyranny of the human face. So, if a lie can for the moment save him, there is absolutely no question that he'll use it. Lie, and deal with the outcome later – it is not proven that this will be any worse than the consequences of the truth. Given an inexhaustible imagination – and Basil has such a one – the realm of lies can be expanded indefinitely.

Basil does not admit the existence of mechanical cause and effect. Everything is will operating on will. If the car won't start it's because it doesn't want to start, and it consequently gets a well-deserved thrashing for disobeying the orders of its master (Gourmet Night). The nail that holds up the moose head doesn't simply give way, nor do the antlers: they *want* to harm him. If this kind of explanation holds true for him in the case of inanimate objects, then imagine how much more ill-intended humans must be, who are palpably and deliberately ranged against him! Compare for instance his reaction to the squatting Mr. Lloyd. Surprised by his sudden appearance out of the blue, Basil for a split second sees himself haunted by the spectre of 'Sybilline' revenge and makes as if to hit him, "I'm so sorry – my wife made a most dreadful mistake". Mr. Lloyd: "Yes, I think she probably did."

In modern anthropological terms, Basil's typical reaction to objects is sometimes described as animistic – pertaining to the primitive religious idea that everything around us possesses an individual soul which is alive and potentially harmful. A tree, a car, a screwdriver, a garden gnome, all possess the dangerous kind of power which the same anthropologists call *mana*, the capacity in a soul to take over another soul and make it subservient to its own will. Basil lives in constant fear of succumbing to the malefic soul of an object (being). His ceaseless lying is by way of reaction to the danger he detects all around him. No sooner has he gained a little respite than some doorpost aims a blow at his head, or a piece of paper purely by its own volition slips out of his hand.

In terms of pure reason, Basil 'knows' that it probably isn't the paper that wants to go, but his own hand that involuntarily releases it. But in his ruthless subjectivity he cannot see any reason why he should have wanted to let go of the paper, so the paper itself must in the last instance be held responsible for its own wilful action. Basil suspects that a unanimous malevolence towards himself has been conferred upon all objects in his vicinity by some dark power, and he is often to be found furiously shaking his fist at a being above. Sometimes, as in The Germans, this demoniac figure takes on the temporal aspect of Harold Wilson, under whose leadership strikes and industrial chaos abounded in 1960s Britain – "Bloody Wilson!" In Communication Problems he for once believes that the supreme being is on his side and tries to kiss him in the air in an act of incredulous gratitude.

Thus, to lie every now and then is no more than a rather muted response to inimical fate. And this is the main reason why Basil always considers his lies as harmless as they are few. (To us and to his intimates, however, they add up to a very substantial number indeed.) Even though Basil's habitual lying originates in his fear and disgust of having to defend actions he knows beforehand will be criticised by Sybil, it does not always hide the truth from her, or at least not just from her. Sometimes, as in Basil the Rat,

The Kipper and the Corpse and Waldorf Salad, Sybil herself is more or less part of his current scam.

But let us now flesh out the story and reveal the anatomy of the formidable lies meant to deceive Sybil, and Sybil alone. In The Builders, Sybil, seized by a vague suspicion that everything is not quite as it should be on the building front, enters the lobby where O'Reilly's (and consequently Basil's) men have obviously got everything wrong. Basil, realising that he won't be able to prevent Sybil from seeing the debacle, pretends to contemplate the scene of destruction.

*Basil: There! Look at that! That's Stubbs for you. Mind you, I warned you! But still – a reputable builder like that! Choh! Tch, tch, tch.*

*Sybil: Stubbs?*

*Basil: Wicked. Tch.*

*Sybil: Where's O'Reilly, Basil?*

*Basil:* (to himself) *Criminal!* (to Sybil) *Hmmm?*

*Sybil: Where's O'Reilly?*

*Basil: O'Reilly?*

*Sybil: Yes, O'Reilly.*

*Basil: Sybil, you never cease to amaze me. Just because of this, you automatically assume that it has to be O'Reilly. You just assume that I have been lying all along! I mean, why O'Reilly?*

*Sybil: Because his van is outside.*

Now, suppose you are in Basil's place. The past can't be changed – you have in fact hired O'Reilly – and you have deliberately deceived Sybil by hiring a builder she loathes from the bottom of her heart. What would you do? Tell her, "I'm so sorry. I made a mistake?" Hardly possible – there have been just too many mistakes.

Would you accuse Polly or Manuel of causing the mishap? A moot point, since O'Reilly wasn't supposed to be there in the first place.

Would you accept a beating-up, then watch how Sybil deals with O'Reilly, knowing that he only has to endure this humiliation once in his life. In the next second he will be out of it – whereas you …

What is preferable? The end effect will be the same. The question is not if but when the demon-wife will go on the rampage. Tell another lie and there's still the ghost of a chance that you may get away with it, if only Sybil's mounting suspicion can be allayed. For a brief moment, Basil is inclined to believe in the possibility of such a miracle. He decides to gamble.

*Basil: Well, he's here now! Of course he's here now! He's come to clear up the mess that your Stubbs has made. That's why* (in a passion) *HIS VAN'S OUTSIDE!* (and throwing down his last card) *On a Sunday! That's what I call service.*

*Sybil: I agree.*

*Basil: You do?*

His surprise is no less than ours. But he's soon brought back down on earth.

*Sybil: Yes. But if Stubbs has made this mess then I think he should come and clear it up.*

Basil keeps his war-wounded leg in reserve for combat to the death, knowing that Sybil for some reason always gets worried when she sees him ostensibly in pain (this, and "George has left Audrey again" always buy him a fraction of time to think).

*Basil: Well, yes – but there's no point now that O'Reilly's here, dear. We want it done straight away.*

*Sybil:* (with devastating logic) *There's no point in paying money to Mr. O'Reilly when Mr. Stubbs would have to do it for free. I'll call him now.*

*Basil: He won't be there on a Sunday.*

*Sybil: Well, then I'll call him at home.*

(Basil is suddenly racked by a spasm of pain from his old war wound.)

The battle is lost, but Polly refuses to deliver the dying emperor to the enemy, knowing that he has to win or she'll go down with him. Sybil catches her in the middle of her Mickey Mouse impression like a fat cat, just reaching its paw out to kill its prey.

*Polly: So you see, we couldn't possibly manage it for at least three weeks, so if you want it done straight away, you'd better try someone like ... oh, what's his name?*

*Sybil:* (overhearing Polly's impersonation in the office) *O'Reilly.*

*Basil:* (refusing to face the bitter facts) *Is that somebody there trying to pretend that they're from Mr. Stubbs' Company? What sort of game do you think you are playing? I mean, really!* (slams down phone, and, to Sybil)*, Would you believe what some of these people will do, Sybil?*

Just imagine the kind of madness which could have resulted from Sybil's allowing him to stray into that particular jungle! But she doesn't. He's dead.

*Sybil: I am going to make you regret this for the rest of your life, Basil.*

And she will. Still, Basil refuses to realise that he is defeated. After Waterloo, Napoleon was tempted to rally the remains of his troops and march against the Prussian army outside Paris, but he capitulated after having calculated the odds. Basil doesn't calculate odds, and it is a sinister pleasure to imagine what he would have had to say for himself upon re-entering the dragon's den, carrying the garden gnome, now stained with blood, in his arms.

★

Communication Problems is another one of those legendary episodes in which Basil tries everything possible to have things his own way while simultaneously keeping the truth from Sybil. The absolute necessity of keeping his gambling secret is the result of Sybil's threat to cut off his private parts on the spot if she ever again catches him squandering their money on the horses.

*Sybil: If I find out the money on that horse was yours, you know what I'll do, Basil.*

*Basil: You'll have to sew 'em back on first.*

The name of the winning horse, Dragonfly, doesn't have dragon in it for nothing. It did win all right but in the end Basil only got the flying part. I hope I'm not exaggerating the crudeness of the scene in which Polly tries to guess the horse's name from Basil's charade behind Sybil's back, by pointing out that the first word that comes to Polly's mind as Basil points to his fly, is 'small'.

The whole episode is actually centred on the notion (and reality) of dragons. To everyone concerned the presence of Mrs. Richards equals that of some kind of fire-breathing monster. Add to this the scene preceding Basil's introduction. To clarify this transition and all the symbolic points, we would do well to remind ourselves of the entire sequence.

*The Major: Going to have a flutter, Fawlty?*

*Basil: No-o, no, no …*

*Sybil: No, Basil doesn't bet any more, Major. Do you, dear?*

*Basil: No dear, I don't. No, that particular avenue of pleasure has been closed off.*

*Sybil:*(quietish) *And we don't want it opened again, do we Basil?* (she goes into the office)

*Basil: No, you don't, dear, no. The Great Warning – Off of May 8th. Yes. Good old St. George, eh, Major?*

*The Major: Hmmm?*

*Basil: He killed a hideous fire-breathing dragon, didn't he, Polly?*

*Polly:* (possibly thinking of Mrs. Richards) *Ran it through with a lance, I believe.*

*Manuel:* (running in) *Mr. Fawlty, Mr. Fawlty. Is Mrs. Er... Room no like ... She want to speak to you... Is problem.*

*Basil:* (moving off) *Ever see my wife making toast, Polly?* (He mimes breathing on both sides of a piece of bread.)

*The Major: Why did he kill it anyway, Fawlty?*

*Basil: I don't know, Major. Better than marrying it.* (He follows Manuel upstairs.)

*The Major:* (with disarming candour) *Marrying it? But he didn't have to kill it though, did he? I mean, he could have just not turned up at the church.* (If only Basil had got that advice fifteen years ago!)

Now Basil finds himself face to face with yet another fire-breathing dragon, which will join Sybil in her effort to count him out for the rest of his life.[11] The final irony of it all is that the beautiful oriental vase, the breaking of which mercilessly signals the end of Basil's dream

---

11  Incidentally, the three-headed, winged mechanical monster that serves as the vehicle and instrument of vengeance to the King of the Moon in Terry Gilliam's film *The Adventures of Baron Münchausen*, answers to the name of Sybil ...

of success, was of course lavishly decorated with Chinese dragons. The dragonfly, on the other hand, symbol of freedom and beauty, is a strange and surprising being. It is able to fly without flying, as if suspended in mid-air. Its irregular movements are conducive to dreamy, irrational moods, and it is, alas, short-lived. Sometimes its life spans less than a day – "Say goodbye to the folks, Gracie ..."

In the matter of those of his lies in which Sybil is more or less his accomplice, Basil, knowing his back is covered, acts with a good deal of self-confidence. For instance, on discovering that members of his staff have been deceiving him (Basil the Rat), he says, "Well, let's have a little Basil hunt, shall we? And then we'll deal with the sackings later!"

The Kipper and the Corpse and Gourmet Night represent other instances of joint efforts to conceal the truth. Waldorf Salad can to some extent be included in the same category. When Sybil finds out the truth behind the missing ingredients of the famous salad, she starts helping Basil instead of making a fuss (well, she does just a little, but that goes without saying, doesn't it?). But we must remember that she hasn't realised that Terry did not threaten to leave, as Basil claims he did. He, Terry, merely wanted a fair share of the £20 Mr. Hamilton gave to Basil to make sure the kitchen stayed open.

The facts of that transaction are not revealed in the course of this episode, but it may be surmised that Sybil would have asked Terry the day after why he didn't stay and prepare dinner for two late guests, especially as they paid £20 for the favour. As soon as Terry told her the truth – and there is no reason to suspect that he would conceal the matter of the Finnish blonde from Mrs. Fawlty – Basil's head would no longer rest safely on his shoulders.

But then again, we don't know the limit of Sybil's own greed. Had she been able to force Basil to hand over the £20, she might have settled for a compromise, paid some money to Terry and kept the rest for herself. It is also possible, perhaps probable, that she would have forced Basil to reimburse the Hamiltons as they were on their way out to their waiting taxi – though, to be sure, not before she had deducted the cost of the meal.[12]

Most of Basil's other lies serve the general purpose of supporting a previous lie which is about to be exposed as such and thus destroy its creator. As often happens when we try to set right a mistake, the damage gets worse. In most cases, the best thing to do is to let errors and insults heal by themselves, unless, of course we are able to make amends right away. Basil can't do that. He gets himself caught in a net, and the more he tries to free himself the more he is enmeshed: the net tightens and tightens until he simply has no room at all for manœuvre.

The portrayal of the maladroit person, unable to solve practical problems rationally, or contriving far too elaborate solutions (one of Rowan Atkinson's specialities as Mr. Bean) is a classic feature of comedy, and at bottom a clown's routine. Basil, or rather John Cleese, is just such a clown, but the special ingenuity of his act lies in the fact that falling off ladders, getting hit by moose heads and saucepans, and aiming blows at imaginary enemies, represent only the visible aspect of a much more complex, invisible and mental problem. This is what makes the humour of the series so much more sophisticated and intellectual than most other comedies based on one or two elementary factors. To see Manuel and Basil messing things up and hitting each other in various ways is enjoy-

---

[12] Like most small-minded shopkeepers, Sybil is meticulous on this point. To her the omission of a breakfast charge to the deceased Mr. Leeman seems an almost frivolous act, and she only decides to go through with it to avoid further attention being brought to the specific circumstances under which Mr. Leeman was found dead (The Kipper and the Corpse).

able even for children – although children may not register the subtleties underlying this incredible universe in which, as in a dream, even seemingly solid cliché becomes unfathomable complication.

In other words, Fawlty Towers, like every genuine piece of art, is enjoyable on many different levels. The development of a simultaneous perception of these levels enhances the viewing pleasure. Take for example the ultimate scene in The Hotel Inspectors. Superficially the pie-in-the-face act is as old as Methuselah (no, no, no *Meth-u-se-lah*, the Biblical figure, never mind … I'll explain later) and an ideal entertainment for five-year-old kids. But when Basil does it, it isn't at all the same as when Laurel and Hardy do it. It has its own symbolism, – "And what can I do for you three gentlemen?" – there really are black holes in the universe …

# THE MONEY AND GAMBLING OBSESSION

THE PRINCIPAL THEME OF A Touch of Class is Basil's attempt to attract not just a better kind but specifically a higher social class of clientele to the Towers. But although he may want to exclude common people, and with them all things vulgar, it does not strike him as incongruous that there's still a Las Vegas-type one-arm bandit in the hotel lounge. Unless Sybil is to blame for this offence against a better class of taste, this calls for an explanation.

The gaming machine, though it's unable to provide financial gain for Basil, reminds him how in the old days he used to thrill to the challenge of a wager of any kind. The machine is much like a religious relic to him, a reminder of the golden days when he could win a small fortune at the races in the afternoon and lose it all at poker in the evening.

Soon after they were married, Sybil began to suspect that the drain on her purse had some connection with Basil's many dubious investments, the majority of which failed to generate any kind of profit. One day she caught him in the act of rifling through her handbag. He tried to explain this away, pretending that he was looking for a tissue on which to blow his stuffed nose, but Sybil forced him to open the hand where the handkerchief supposedly was, and found a £10 note.

So when Lord Melbury asks Basil to cash him a cheque for

£200, Basil is at first overwhelmed by the size of the sum, but then quickly slips into his old habit of regarding large sums of money as coming and going at will. The £40 spent on the advertisement in *Country Life* is in the same way a mere trifle, whereas paying a few pounds extra to have Stubbs replace the doors in the lobby seems outrageous, because he would actually get something material in return for the money invested.

It is only when the sums are small that Basil dismounts from his high horse. He interrogates Mr. Macintosh at great length before he allows 32 pence, wrongly charged in the first place, to be deducted from his bill, whereas the offer of £87.000 made to Mrs. Richards for her house in Brighton just makes him yawn (Communication Problems). Polly's request for a loan of £100 to make up the money she needs to buy a car almost causes a stab of pain. The extra £20 he makes in Waldorf Salad is manna from heaven to him, but doesn't stop him delivering his speech on the idealism of the English, as if it were in fact he who had given Mr. Hamilton the money to stay in the dining-room after chef had left, and not vice versa.

Having to replace a corked bottle of the Corton for a guest who doesn't have a title ("Didn't you see, I just uncorked it?" "No, no, the wine has reacted with the cork, and gone bad.") brings out the Scrooge in Basil, "All right, then, but it'll cost me." When he and Sybil are about to leave for their round of golf in Paignton (The Builders), Basil starts removing note after note from the cash box, to be interrupted by his wife who takes the whole lot from him, returning a single fiver. The irony of Basil's tacit acceptance of her actions (she takes the box away from him, locks it, takes out the key and places it under the reception counter) is best appreciated as we remember his penchant for throwing money around like confetti.

Like so many women who fall in love with gamblers, Sybil thought that the strength of her love would be able to cure him of his vice. She had to pay dearly for this naiveté. Tranquillity would not be forthcoming until she made up her mind about which course of action to take. To curb this evil she must crush the serpent under her heel.

Basil, however, keeps on trying to deceive her. The power of his gambling obsession is in fact equal to that of his fear of being found out by the old trouble and strife. As we have seen, this is also the reason why his defeat in Communication Problems is so devastating and final, just when, for once, he had decided to save his winnings, even to bank them. Which brings us to the last and most crucial of Basil Fawlty's mental hangups.

# THE SYBILOPHOBIA, OR JUST: SYBILIS

BASIL HAS ALL THE reason in the world to fear his wife. But he is also indebted to her for still being alive. It is certain that he would have been a ruined man on the very brink of suicide had not Sybil put an end to his gambling habit. As it is, Basil is constantly on the brink of a complete mental breakdown. Maybe he recognises, deep down, that he is his own worst enemy, and that the only person capable of saving him from himself is Sybil. This of course doesn't prevent him from wanting her out of the way, yet he always finds himself up against her frightening omnipresence.

The bedroom scene of the married couple in The Wedding Party is a case in point. Sybil, her hair in curlers and dressed in a fluorescent purple negligée that matches her nail varnish and clashes violently with the lemon-yellow bedspread, is lying in bed (we note that Sybil and Basil don't share a double bed). She is simultaneously reading a comic strip (I swear, take a close look!), eating chocolates from a large box and smoking a cigarette, while from time to time emitting her characteristic, seal-like bark of enjoyment. Whenever the chocolate centre proves to be a kind she doesn't care for – nut or cherry – she takes the offending piece out of her mouth and places it in the ashtray on the night-table between the beds. Basil, reading *Jaws* (not the one by Shakespeare) watches her in disgust. The horror of the scene becomes complete when Audrey telephones.

Sybil's sibilant "Yes, I know," repeated *ad infinitum* and, "He doesn't deserve you. He really doesn't", consummate the Basilean hell. He tries to escape it by clasping his hands over his ears. In vain. Sybil is so perfectly herself, and so much 'at home', that Basil feels compelled to get up and leave the bedroom.

I would like to ask the male reader: How would you react if you had to endure the same shameless and vulgar banality? Would you lie there trying to take an interest in the conversation? Would you search for earplugs? Or would you, as Basil does, intervene and try to put an end to the torture by asking the 'bleeding obvious,' "If you know, why is she telling you then?"

Let's assess the situation. In this scene and context Sybil is a perfect horror. In an identical situation, I personally would be sorely tempted to strangle her with my bare hands. I can hardly imagine anything more dreadful than having to share this sort of intimacy with any person, let alone the woman of my choice. Basil's reading *Jaws* is a pertinent illustration of his terrible dilemma – he can't get rid of Sybil, only dream of fatal accidents – and his fantasies constantly run along these lines. We have already heard, in this episode's opening scene, his rhetorical question (to Major Gowen and Mrs. Peignoir), "Did you ever see that film *How to Murder your Wife?* … Awfully good, I saw it six times."

Of course, Basil knows that he is quite unable to do away with Sybil, and that, just supposing that he succeeded in doing so, he knows also that he will forever be haunted by her. English law is another deterrent, as is his fatalistic conformity to his marriage vows. So there he is – stuck. The only course open to him, once he has accepted the inevitability of his situation, is to try to keep his opponent unaware of his secret ways of getting through the day. This continuous deception naturally gives rise to a corresponding fear of being found out and punished by this implacable instrument of the forces of darkness.

So, hand in hand with Basil's racism, snobbery and sexual repression, goes his misogyny. Although sometimes in its outward aspect apparently benevolent (he sometimes *can* be amiable toward women), it in the end always betrays itself in his conviction that the female sex and intelligence are mutually exclusive – a contradiction in terms, in fact. The Wedding Party is rich in deprecatory remarks that form a continuous counterpoint to the theme of Basil's obsession with what he believes to be the inconceivably perverted activities going on in his hotel. We have for instance his apology to the Lloyd family, "I'm sorry but my wife has made a mistake … you know what women are like, they've only got one brain between the lot of them."

Or take the dialogue between the Major and Basil occasioned by Sybil's leaving to visit Audrey.

*The Major: You don't like Audrey very much, do you?*

*Basil: Oh, dreadful woman. Dreadful.*

*The Major: Well, I think it is very decent of your wife to go round there and listen to all that rubbish.*

*Basil: Couldn't do without it, Major.*

*The Major: She's a fine woman – Mrs. Fawlty.*

*Basil: No, no, I wouldn't say that.*

*The Major: No, nor would I …*

In The Germans, Basil and the Major have another conversation in which a tendency to confound women with 'inferior' races in general emerges. As we relish this scene, we must remember that to the Major the word 'nigger' simply describes a person from the continent of Africa, whereas to Basil the term is less unequivocal. However, Basil is in no way intimidated by the Major's clear-cut racial distinctions. We enter the dialogue just after the Major has explained that he once took an attractive woman to see a cricket match at the Oval.

*The Major: And the strange thing was … throughout the morning she kept referring to the Indians as 'niggers'. "No, no, no," I said, "The niggers are the West Indians. These people are wogs." "No, no," she said, "All cricketers are niggers."*

*Basil: They do get awfully confused, don't they? They're not thinkers. I see it with Sybil every day.*

*The Major: … I do wish I could remember her name. She's still got my wallet.*

*Basil: As I was saying, no capacity for logical thought.*

*The Major: Who?*

*Basil: Women.*

*The Major: Oh yes, yes. I thought you meant Indians.*

*Basil: No, no, no, no – wasn't it Oscar Wilde who said, "They have minds like Swiss cheese?"*

*The Major: What do you mean – hard?*

*Basil: No, no – full of holes.*

*The Major: Really? … Indians?*

*Basil: No, women!*

*The Major: Oh.*

A conversation containing direct statements and allusions of this kind would probably be out of the question on any American TV show either in 1975 or the present day. Indeed, it would have a very hard time getting past the censors of today's BBC as well. In modern American films the word 'nigger' is rather like a death sentence put in the mouth of a future victim; anyone denigrating people in this way is destined to come to a very sticky end indeed when justice is finally done.

But humour is a different genre, in which such taboos can sometimes be broken. The Monty Python crew were the first in the history of entertainment to have the rare privilege of making fun of anything they considered worth making fun of – Scots and Norwegians not excluded. In Fawlty Towers this privilege was accorded to John Cleese personally. By making Basil the ultimate victim of his own prejudices, Cleese was able to get away with quite a few illiberalities, disguised as they were in illustrious slapstick. But the hard core of the shows remains an impressive testimony to the freedom of thought and expression that obtained within the series.[13]

Basil doesn't know the quotation, since he's never read the book from which it comes, but he would very much find to his liking the French poet Baudelaire's disenchanted remark: "Woman is natural, thus abominable." To Basil, a woman is just another kind of savage, capable of domestication perhaps, but impossible to educate. This is why Basil refuses to recognise any value in the intellectual accomplishments (foreign-language skills, for example) he sometimes finds among women and other primitive beings (guests).

Having this generally low opinion of women, Basil fears the savage brutality of female vengeance too. It is only natural that Basil, on account of his strong conscious aversion to women, should be preoccupied with unconscious sexual fantasies of the most disturbing kind. These are those that manifest themselves in his frantic purges among the guests for suspected breaches of Victorian decency. And, as we have seen, although he hardly raises an eyebrow on observing his wife flirting with a guest, he himself is seized by the most powerful agitation as soon as any woman makes the slightest pass at him.

Toward the end of The Wedding Party, his imagination has become so fevered that he falls prey to phantoms of his own making. The prospect of a Mrs. Peignoir breaking down his bedroom door, wrestling him onto the bed, and trying to "sit on him again", is so horrifying that he must invent a story about Sybil's unexpected re-

---

[13] Even today I can't imagine anyone other than a Monty Python member publicly pulling off the kind of joke that Eric Idle did in connection with the official Monty Python reunion in Aspen, Colorado some years ago. Before a large live and television audience, he related the event when the Monty Pythons, invited to produce a comedy for a German TV channel, were taken sightseeing by their hosts to visit the concentration camp in Dachau (I guess they thought it would put them in a creative mood!). As it was already late afternoon, it was feared that the premises might be closed when they arrived there. Somebody in the group then suggested: "Tell them we're Jewish."

By the way, Cleese himself later had to atone for his racial derring-do in Fawlty Towers. In a Western film from 1985, Silverado, with among others Kevin Kline and Kevin Costner in the leading roles, Cleese himself appears in the role of Sheriff Langston. When a bar owner complains that "the nigger destroyed my bar", the sheriff cuts him short, saying, "I don't very much like that word, Carter." After that conversion to terminological decency, John Cleese has been considered kosher even with the Freemasons of Santa Barbara, and can nowadays be seen golfing with the city's leading Rotarians.

turn – "I think you'll find it on the second shelf, Sybil darling."
(We note that the standard "dear" is replaced here by the desperate
and excessively fond "darling.")

It would be an exaggeration to say that Basil is constantly in fear
of getting caught *in flagrante delicto*. He is far too inhibited even to
flirt with women, let alone try to get into bed with them. He is
however desperately afraid of getting caught out in his most secret
fantasies, which surely include scenarios in which he is unfaithful
to Sybil and ultimately makes her the victim of a fatal accident.[14]

This constant wishful plotting against the dragon-wife naturally leaves a sense of guilt. The "Yes, dear", which so many married men find to be their passport to tranquillity, only partly works
in Sybil's case. She is much too suspicious and stubborn to let him
get away with mere phrases. She wants to see things done, and she
is very demanding. There is nothing in the series to suggest that
Sybil does actually work quite as hard as she would have us believe.
As a matter of fact, she is mostly gossiping with someone – preferably with Audrey, and about men – or with guests, as at the beginning of The Kipper and the Corpse, everybody else on the staff
is busy serving lunch, while Sybil has all the time in the world to
explain to Mr. Libson that, "We all need our privacy."

---

14 For psychological illustration in this regard I shall have to refer the reader to the film *A
Fish called Wanda* (1988) where the script allows Archie (John Cleese), initially caught in a
similar Victorian strait-jacket, to actually break loose from his dreaded wife and satisfy his
heart's desire.

15 There is indeed a conspicuous lack of staff in the hotel. In Communication Problems,
Sybil asks Polly if she has time to give a hand with the cleaning of the rooms. This suggests
that there is someone else doing the rooms normally. Unless we are to assume that this person is Manuel, or even that Basil and Sybil take turns making beds and cleaning bathrooms,
this leaves us with the alternatives that the rooms are either mysteriously made by themselves, or that there is in fact some very discreet member of the hotel staff that we never encounter or hear anything about.

She takes special delight in assigning new tasks to Basil, and more often than not delegates her own work to someone else.[15] The cry, "Basil! Basil!! Basil!!!" is a strident alarm signal that reverberates throughout the series. Basil himself has become inured to the mastiff bellowing, and finds nothing exceptional in her normal tone of voice. As long as she hasn't worked herself up to a real frenzy (as in the closing scene of The Kipper and the Corpse) he keeps teasing her from the other side of the fence. However, whenever Sybil shows the claw, Basil comes running, tail between his legs. It always works. He's in mortal fear of her tiger's roar. She really has him under her thumb. It doesn't make him any more efficient – or a better husband for that matter – but it affords her a vicarious pleasure in the absence of the most vital marital fulfilment.

Basil himself has no idea of how to change things for the better, and prefers to invent endless compromises, lies and escape routes, which all in the end leave him surrounded, painted into a corner, nailed to the wall. But although Sybil has burned him alive many times, he is always just about able to rise, it seems, like a pitiable phoenix from the ashes of his humiliation. And though he knows in his heart that he will always be found out in the end, yet still he dreams of the day when he'll outwit her once and for all. What this will entail he doesn't quite dare to envisage. But we may be certain that if it ever comes to it, his tears at Sybil's funeral, his woebegone leaning on Polly and his forlorn embracing of Manuel, will have every appearance of sincerity.

Up yours, Bas!

# THE SECONDARY CHARACTERS

# 3

WE HAVE NOW AT some length discussed the principal and, so to speak, perennial actors in the series. The time has come to take a closer look at the people who come and go in various episodes. Most of these are temporary guests, either staying in the hotel, or coming to lunch or dinner. There are also people who visit the Towers for other reasons – builders, delivery men, inspectors, friends, and the like.

The great majority of the actors playing these auxiliary roles appear just once during the course of the twelve episodes, meaning that they take part in one episode and so only have one identity. There are three exceptions, however. One of these, and a very interesting one too, is Terence Connolly, who incarnates Mr. Wearing in the first episode of A Touch of Class, and Mr. Johnstone in Waldorf Salad. In both instances he plays probably the most abused and insulted of all the guests at the Towers. It is true that both Lord Melbury and Mr. Hutchison are ultimately more humiliated than he, but in their cases there is some partial justification of Basil's actions, whereas Mr. Wearing and Mr. Johnstone suffer his extreme discourtesy at the slightest provocation. In A Touch of Class, Mr. Wearing's sole transgression is his repeated order from inside the bar, "A gin and orange, a lemon squash and a Scotch and water." In Waldorf Salad he does no more than inform Basil that his wife's prawns were inedible and the charge ought to be deducted from the bill. That's all he does, but he receives worse treatment than a dog in the street for it.

An interesting detail is that although Mr. Wearing appears with a well defined bald patch in A Touch of Class, Mr. Johnstone in Waldorf Salad, filmed five years later, has quite a full head of hair! Is this to be attributed to the stunning efficiency of Regain, or are we to assume that his new coiffure is in fact a Robin Hood hairstyle – "take from the rich and give to the poor?" It seems that John Cleese and Terence Connolly got on well with one another in real life, as the latter also had a small part in the 1997 motion picture *Fierce Creatures*, directed, produced and starred in by John Cleese, in which the action, *naturellement*, takes place in a zoo …

The second person to visit the Towers twice is actress Elizabeth Henson, who makes a rather fierce appearance as the indulgent mother of the spoiled brat who gives Basil a hard time at the beginning of Gourmet Night. She was to return in The Kipper and the Corpse as the more reserved and timid character Mrs. White, who with her husband in vain tries to get into their room while Basil props up the dead body of Mr. Leeman in their wardrobe.

The only other subsidiary character to appear twice in the series is the delivery man. In The Builders his name is Kerr, and his role in this episode is to deliver the charming garden gnome to 16 Elwood Avenue ("Yeah, with a bath, you dago twit"). In Communication Problems, this actor, Barney Dorman, performs exactly the same function as he does in The Builders, but his name is given as Bennion in the script. Here he brings Mrs. Richards her beautiful oriental vase and the glove with £90 inside – in an euphoric instant capable, as it were, of putting an end to Basil's lifelong run of bad luck. We may suspect that the same delivery man – whether called Kerr, Bennion or something else – was also responsible for bringing the moose head into Basil's ambit (The Germans). If so, the shop from which all three items were purchased must by deduction be Samson's in town.

All other secondary characters only appear once. Naturally, some of these take roles absolutely indispensable to the episodes in which they appear – for example, Lord Melbury and Danny in A Touch of Class, O'Reilly in The Builders, Mr. Walt and Mr. Hutchison in The Hotel Inspectors, Alan, Jean and Mrs. Peignoir in The Wedding Party, Mrs. Richards in Communication Problems, Mr. Johnson, Miss Miles and the doctors Abbott in The Psychiatrist, Mr. and Mrs. Hamilton in Waldorf Salad, Mr. Carnegie in Basil the Rat (his monologue on the inadequacy of the Fawlty kitchen is a marvel!), Dr. Price and, of course, Mr. Leeman (who, paradoxically, acts dead throughout the greater part of his appearance) in The Kipper and the Corpse.

The remaining secondary roles are of a more transitory character, but are crucial. For instance, in Basil the Rat the action would be weakened without the phlegmatic yet muted sonority of Mr. Taylor's only line, "One bottle of the Beaujolais, please." Mrs. Chase, cuddling her lap-dog, nicely sets the tone for The Kipper and the Corpse. Roger's, "Up yours, Bas!" in The Anniversary is perfectly authentic, as is Mr. Firkins', "There's a very nice little filly running at Exeter this afternoon" in Communication Problems. André's conciliatory, "Oh, there's always a few" to Basil's indignant observation, "So much for tonight's guests. Ignorant rabble." (Gourmet Night), has the same low-key charm as Mr. Mackintosh's Scottish frugality in, "Drinks? Me?" (Communication Problems), or Lurphy's musically intoned, "Thick as a plank," in reference to Manuel's hysterical repetition of "orelly men." (The Builders).

Of special interest is the brief appearance of actor Charles McKeown, whose connection with the Monty Python circle was through his collaboration with Terry Gilliam and playwright Tom Stoppard on the manuscript of the devastatingly dystopic cult film

*Brazil*. The same Charles McKeown later had a hand in scriptwriting Gilliam's superb drama-comedy *The Adventures of Baron Münchausen*, and played the part in the film of the Baron's servant Adolphus, the bespectacled man in the black cape who could hit any target, no matter how distant, with his rifle.

McKeown's appearance in Fawlty Towers is so brief as to pass practically unnoticed. While Basil and Manuel are frantically trying to hide the body of Mr. Leeman in The Kipper and the Corpse, a certain Mr. Ingrams, waiting at the front desk for Sybil to give him the key to his room, says, "Thank you". This is his only line. The next time we see him we hardly notice who he is. In a desperate attempt to find a place to hide the body until the undertakers arrive, Polly flings the door open to Room 8, and the whole party – the corpse dangling between Manuel and Basil – is quite surprised to see Mr. Ingrams blowing up his sex-aid doll. But at this point of general excitement, not to say panic, Basil himself hasn't the time or inclination to embark on another tirade against the licentious mores of his guests – on the contrary, he even apologises for the intrusion.

The episodes in which the largest number of secondary characters appear must be The Germans, where Basil's fire-drill obliges every guest in the hotel to assemble in the lobby, and Waldorf Salad, where there is a similar round-up of potentially hostile individuals. However, in both instances the secondary characters have nothing much of dramatic significance to do. They remain mere spectators of Basil's assumption of superhuman stature as he fills the screen with his presence – "This is exactly how Nazi Germany started …"

In connection with our examination of the script itself and of the series as theatre, we observe a return to the old and reliable dramaturgical device of a last act that ends with all the actors on stage. This is notably the case in Waldorf Salad and especially so in The

Kipper and the Corpse, where practically everyone who has participated in the episode – and perhaps a few others! – is gathered in the lobby to witness the protagonist's taking refuge in a laundry basket that is to be loaded into a lorry on its way to its next collection.

Since in *The Worshipper's Companion* many of the auxiliary characters are appropriately referred to at the precise points where they cross the path of the protagonist, I shall not burden the reader with a redundant list of who they are and in what episode they appear. On the other hand, those readers who seek information about a specific guest actor's credentials outside the homoncular insulation characteristic of his existence within the Towers, the best standard reference, to my knowledge, is *Fawlty Towers Fully Booked*, which has devoted a special entry to the official careers of each and every one of these talented, if sometimes only briefly appearing, actors.

# 4

## THE BLEEDING UNOBVIOUS

THE FAWLTY TOWERS SERIES contains a good deal of not-so-obvious references to illustrious characters, celebrities of the day, historical events and other social phenomena. In this chapter we shall shed some light upon the allusions that make up such a vital part of Basil's private musings. These are often ignored or simply not understood by the people around him, and on this account likely on occasion to elude audiences as well.

Let us begin with Basil's comment to Sybil as she is about to open the briefcase which Lord Melbury has deposited in their safe (A Touch of Class). "I never thought I would live to see the day when a peer of the realm entrusts to us a case of valuables." To British viewers a *peer of the realm* of course represents a perfectly understood social distinction. Viewers in other countries might on the other hand find it useful to know that the phrase usually refers to a person entitled to sit in the House of Lords – the aristocratic body that was a vital part of the British parliamentary system.[16]

In The Builders, Basil is determined that someone other than

---

[16] Not all peers sit in the House of Lords, however. There is also the courtesy-title system, where the son of a peer may use one of his subsidiary titles by courtesy only, which does not entitle him to sit. In fact, since the recent reform of the House, the majority of hereditary peers do not sit.

himself must be held responsible for the disastrous 'renovation' of the lobby. Polly, on duty on that occasion, has told Manuel to wake her up as soon as O'Reilly's men arrive. But Manuel, finding her deeply asleep, hasn't the heart to wake her. He thinks he can handle the situation himself. Soon Basil's hysterical investigation into the question of responsibility for the mishap reaches critical mass.

*Polly: It wasn't really his* (Manuel's) *fault.*

*Basil: Well, whose fault was it then, you cloth-eared bint – Denis Compton's?*

Cricket fans with a passion for the history of the game will have no problem identifying that one, but for all the rest of us (and I have reason to believe that there are quite a few of us) it is a riddle. Well, then, Denis Charles Scott Compton was one of the greatest of English cricketers, who died in 1997 at the age of 78. The then prime minister, John Major, expressed the nation's loss and sorrow with unusual emotive force, and a public obituary stated humouristically: "Compton was noted most especially for the poetry of his batting, allied with a certain schoolboy impishness that accompanied his shot selection." There was, in other words, something in Denis Compton's character to suggest that he, given propitious circumstances, could act in the manner of a mischievous child. But to assume some kind of logic at work here on Basil's part may indeed be a moot point. Denis Compton is probably just an example of utter 'unrelatedness' to the scene of the action, that is to say, he is one of the most unlikely persons to have been found present on the premises when O'Reilly's men, under Manuel's supervision, cock everything up. It's simply another instance of Basil's inadvertent 'sledge-hammer' wit. Nonetheless, it should of course be mentioned that Cleese himself devoted himself to cricket during his college years. *Fawlty Towers Fully Booked* contains the following entry, utterly cryptic to people who know next to nothing about cricket (like me) but suggestive and, above all, evocative of said Compton: "In Cleese's last year at college, the team played the mighty MCC and Cleese secured the wicket of the legendary *Denis Compton*: caught Whitty, bowled Cleese for 22."

Amateurs of Pythonesque reference will relish the fact that Denis Compton's name had already been used in a Monty Python show in 1972, featuring a certain Mr. Pither on a bicycle tour of Cornwall. Mr. Pither meets a Mr. Gulliver who turns out to be Lev Bronstein, alias Trotsky, who yearns to return to Russia and resume his role as leader of the Soviet Communist Party. In his inaugural speech at the party rally he soon transmogrifies into Eartha Kitt, singing, "I'm just an old-fashioned girl." Denis Compton is mentioned earlier as being among the celebrities who have signed the autograph album owned by an elderly French couple (John Cleese and Eric Idle) who are camping out in the French *Alpes maritimes.*

In The Germans, after having been thoroughly cross-examined over the telephone by Sybil, Basil sees Manuel re-enter the lobby and exclaims, "Oh, it's the Admirable Crichton." This is an ironic reference to a 1902 play of the same name by Sir James Barrie (the author of the world-famous children's play *Peter Pan*). The plot is about a marvellously resourceful butler who, when shipwrecked on a desert island with his master and his master's family, emerges, by virtue of his skills and the power of his personality, as the natural leader of the group.

Although the Admirable Crichton of the play was an entirely fictional character, there is an historical underpinning to the name. The 'real' Admirable Crichton – thus named because of his swift intellect, vast learning, good looks and prowess in disputation and fencing – was of Scottish noble descent. In 1582 he was ambushed and killed in a coup planned by his own pupil, Vicenzo di Gonzaga, son of the duke of Mantua. James Crichton, already a legend, was only twenty-two years old at the time of his death. That Manuel barely resembles either Crichton goes without saying, but the deliberate inappropriateness is telling.

In The Hotel Inspectors Sybil tries to persuade Basil to try to be a bit more courteous to their guests. Sybil: "This is a hotel Basil, not a Borstal."

British viewers will know that this refers to the first prison specifically for young offenders situated near Borstal in the county of Kent. Later, the borstal system, or simply Borstal, came to signify any correctional institution for young criminals, whether in Kent or any other part of the country.

In The Germans, a fire extinguisher goes off in Basil's face and knocks him out. As he comes to, he finds himself in the same hospital ward as Sybil, and begins to recall the event. He gets quite excited about the unreliability of the emergency equipment. "I mean, what is the point of a fire extinguisher? It sits there for months, and when you actually have a fire, when you actually need the bloody thing it blows your head off!! I mean, what is happening to this country? It's bloody Wilson!"

Younger Fawlty Towers aficionados might find this information pertinent. Harold Wilson succeeded the deceased Labour leader Hugh Gaitskell in 1963 and in the following year, the Labour Party having won the General Election, became prime minister. Harold Wilson's premiership was to last for thirteen years, during which the country was bedevilled by repeated strikes. In 1976 Wilson unexpectedly resigned and James Callaghan became Prime Minister. It was during Callaghan's term that the 'winter of discontent' cast its pall over the country, and the way was left clear for the Conservatives, under Margaret Thatcher, to win the election of 1979. The vehemence of her economic reforms must be seen against the background of the demoralisation brought about by one and a half decades of union action, which occurred mostly during the stewardship of Harold Wilson. This is the reason why the Major always intones, "Another car strike" on first glancing at the newly arrived newspaper. Basil goes a step further and holds Wilson personally responsible for just about anything that goes wrong in society – and in his personal life, too. The weakening of the work ethic, the increased power of the working class, the general decline of society and morals, are all ultimately attributable to a socialist Britain of which Harold Wilson is the symbol.

Even without knowing that The Germans was the last episode in the first series of six shows from 1974, we could deduce that it must be from the fact that Wilson resigned in 1976. In the 1979 series we find a reference to Margaret Thatcher. Mr. Johnson, in The Psychiatrist, compares the guide book *What's on in Torquay?* with other books supposedly "one of the world's shortest", such as *Great English Lovers* or *The Wit of Margaret Thatcher*. Basil is not charmed by Johnson's remark.

Speaking of Johnson, Basil makes the ironic assumption that the woman in Johnson's room is Mrs. (Lady Bird) Johnson, the wife of the late president of the United States, today mostly remembered for his unflinching ambition to crush communist North Vietnam. It is also in this context that we must place the U.S. foreign policy adviser and diplomat Henry Kissinger, to whom reference is made on no fewer than three occasions. The first is in connection with Mr. Hutchison in The Hotel Inspectors. Hutchison: "If anybody wants me, I'll be in the lounge." Basil: "Anyone in particular? ... I mean, Henry Kissinger?" The second reference is in Gourmet Night, when Basil revenges himself for the insults he has to endure from the spoiled brat in the company of his elderly parents in the dining-room. The boy wants ordinary salad cream instead of real mayonnaise. Basil: "Still, I'll tell him (chef) to get some salad cream.

You never know when Henry Kissinger is going to drop in." The third mention of the name appears later in the same episode. Sybil: "Who's out?" Basil: "Kurt! Who do you think – Henry Kissinger?"

Earlier on in this tirade Basil alluded to another celebrity. Mrs. Heath: "May I ask why you don't have proper salad cream. I mean, most restaurants –" Basil: "Well, the chef only buys it on special occasions, you know, gourmet nights and so on, but when he's got a bottle – ah! – he's a genius with it. He can unscrew a cap like Robert Carrier."

Robert Carrier was an American cookery writer who in 1963 became world-famous on the publication of his book, *The Old and the New Classic Great Dishes of the World*. With his subsequent culinary television-performances in Britain during the 1970s, he added to the growing British interest in cookery, at that time still deeply entrenched in the prawn cocktail, steak, chips and salad, Black Forest gateau regimen. In his television shows he excelled in making sumptuous meals – so Basil's reference to his way with a bottle of salad cream may be taken as not only ironic but inappropriate too. Robert Carrier remains to this day a renowned chef and the distinguished author of many cookery books.[17]

Another American celebrity to be alluded to in the series is the actor James (Jimmy) Cagney (1899-1986), who was born on New York's Lower East Side and began his film career in the 1920s. Mr.

---

[17] Acording to Jonathan Margolis, in *Cleese Encounters*, one of the first things John Cleese did, after having been told by Connie Booth in 1977 that he was now free from any matrimonial obligations, was to travel to Hintlesham Hall in Essex to participate in a cookery class led by the said Robert Carrier. I impart this information strictly as an objective point of reference, since it is contrary to my purpose to extend the analyses of the characters of the series to the individuals who created it. Or in Cleese's own words: "Sir Laurence Olivier didn't become Hamlet or Lear just because he acted the roles, did he?" That there might still be a lingering suspicion of a 'guilt by association' is something for which neither I, nor Cleese himself, can be held responsible.

Cagney mostly distinguished himself in 'tough-guy' roles. At the moment when Basil's Hitler impression can no longer be staved off, Polly nevertheless attempts to divert him by shouting, "No, Mr. Fawlty! Do Jimmy Cagney instead." "You dirty rat," etc. (The Germans).

A direct quote from early American sit-com entertainment is Basil's remark to the Major, who once again has some difficulty in understanding what Basil requires from him. Basil: (trying to convey the 'official' version of the rat hunt to the Major) "Yes, and the starling was in the garden and the rat was nowhere at all." The Major: "Well, I didn't see him." Basil: (moving off) "Say good night to the folks, Gracie." This line is taken from the *Burns and Allen Show*, starring George Burns and Gracie Allen, which was very popular in the 1950s-60s. A pivotal feature of the show was Gracie's use of 'feminine' logic, and George's ironic bemusement. The show would end with a torrent of Gracie's 'rationalisations' of the situation built up in the half-hour of each episode. As she ended, George would say the immortal words to her, kindly and long-sufferingly, but meaning to shut her up. Gracie died in the 1960s. George Burns was to become one of America's most enduring senior actors; he kept acting well into his nineties and lived to be over a hundred years old.

Perhaps most intriguing of all the scenes in the series that contain references to celebrities, dead or alive, is the one featured in the following dialogue between Basil and the Major in Communication Problems.

*Basil: Look, you were in your best suit.*

*The Major: Was I? Oh yes, of course – I went to the theatre, of course.*

*Basil: No, no.*

*The Major: Yes, with Winnie Atwell.*

*Basil: Winnie Atwell?*

*The Major: Well, Marjorie Atwell. I always called her Winnie because she looked like Winnie.*

*Basil: She's not black.*

*The Major: Black? Churchill wasn't black.*

It is obvious that the Winnie Atwell referred to here is the colourful and very popular West Indian singer who had such success in Britain during the 1950s and early 1960s. Winnie was likewise the nickname of Winston Churchill. However, I have been utterly unable to find out who *Marjorie* Atwell was. Unless we are simply to read this dialogue as a deliberate piece of obfuscation, there remains, as far as I am able to tell, no other alternative than to suppose that Marjorie Atwell was a person who lived in Torquay, or perhaps acted at a theatre there. She seems to be familiar to both Basil and the Major. In contrast to the West Indian singer, she apparently was Caucasian. Consequently, when Basil infers that the said Marjorie isn't black, the Major's memory again becomes confused. He takes a leap of faith, freely associating black with a Winnie who has now become Churchill, and only him, where Basil's previous statement, "She's not black," relates in his mind to good old 'Winnie', who of course was neither a woman, nor black.

Winnie Atwell was a well-known figure on British television as well, but not all such references are to celebrities of film and television. Some have decidedly more of a British domestic character, and an even larger portion of them are in one way or another of an historical nature. The episode The Kipper and the Corpse is particularly rich in references of these kinds. Mr. Leeman, who is eventually found dead in his bed, hurts Basil's sense of decorum by not responding to his cheerful, "Good night." Sybil defends Leeman, knowing that he didn't feel too well. Basil: "He only had to say 'good night', dear. It's not the Gettysburg Address."

The Gettysburg Address was the famous speech Abraham Lincoln gave on November 19, 1863 to the soldiers who had fought and survived the battle outside Gettysburg, Pennsylvania, against General Robert E. Lee and his Confederate troops. In many ways the victory of the Union at Gettysburg marks a major turning-point in the history of the United States.

Seeing that another car strike is in the headlines, Basil of course cannot refrain from commenting on it while preparing to deliver breakfast to Mr. Leeman, by now stone dead. Basil: (to himself more than anybody else) "Another car strike, would you believe it? They ought to get Butlin's to run our car factories."

Although 'bloody' Wilson was no longer in office when Basil uttered this, the target of his sarcasm remains the same. Butlin's is a British company that owns holiday camps and amusement parks providing holiday makers with "the complete leisure experience". The best elucidation of the implications of his mentioning Butlin's in this context is given by Basil himself in his inadvertent 'funeral address' to Mr. Leeman: "Taxpayers pay 'em millions each year, they get the money, go on strike. It's called socialism. I mean if they don't like making cars why don't they get themselves another bloody job, designing cathedrals or composing viola concertos? The British Leyland Concerto in four movements, all of 'em slow, with a four-hour tea-break in between. I'll tell you why, 'cos they're not interested in anything except lounging about on conveyor belts, stuffing themselves with my money."

He returns to the subjects of leisure and holidays in the very next scene. Just before he's forced to realise that Leeman is irreversibly dead, he still believes that the others are talking about Mrs. Chase's aggressive lap-dog. He says: "What's the matter with that dog?" Manuel: … "He's dead." Basil: "Well, he's certainly struggling for life at the moment. A dead dog in the breakfast room, eh? Egon Ronay'd knock off a star for that."

Egon Ronay is a famous writer on British travel, hotels and restaurants. His Guide is roughly comparable to the French *Guide Michelin*. To have one star removed – if you ever had one – from this guide is to be officially demoted in the hierarchy of tourism.

Military references, such as to the Gettysburg Address, abound throughout the series. The episode we are discussing, The Kipper and the Corpse, uses a reference straight after the Egon Ronay allusion. Dr. Price: (to Basil) "You mean you didn't realise that the man was dead?" Basil: "People don't talk that much in the morning … Well look, I'm just delivering a tray, right? If the guest isn't singing, 'Oh, What a Beautiful Morning' I don't immediately think, 'Oh, there's another one snuffed it in the night – another name in the Fawlty Towers Book of Remembrance, I mean, this is a hotel, not the Burma Railway."

The building of the Burma Railway – also called 'the railway of death' – has been commemorated to great effect in the famous film *The Bridge over the River Kwai*, with Alec Guinness in the principal role. During World War II, prisoners of war, mostly British, were used as forced labour by the Japanese army to complete the construction of a railway from Burma to Thailand. Death by accident, exhaustion, execution and pestilence was rampant. In fact, the entire remaining work-force was probably saved from death by the explosion of the atomic bombs over Hiroshima and Nagasaki in 1945, which forced the capitulation of the Japanese army and the eventual repatriation of its prisoners.

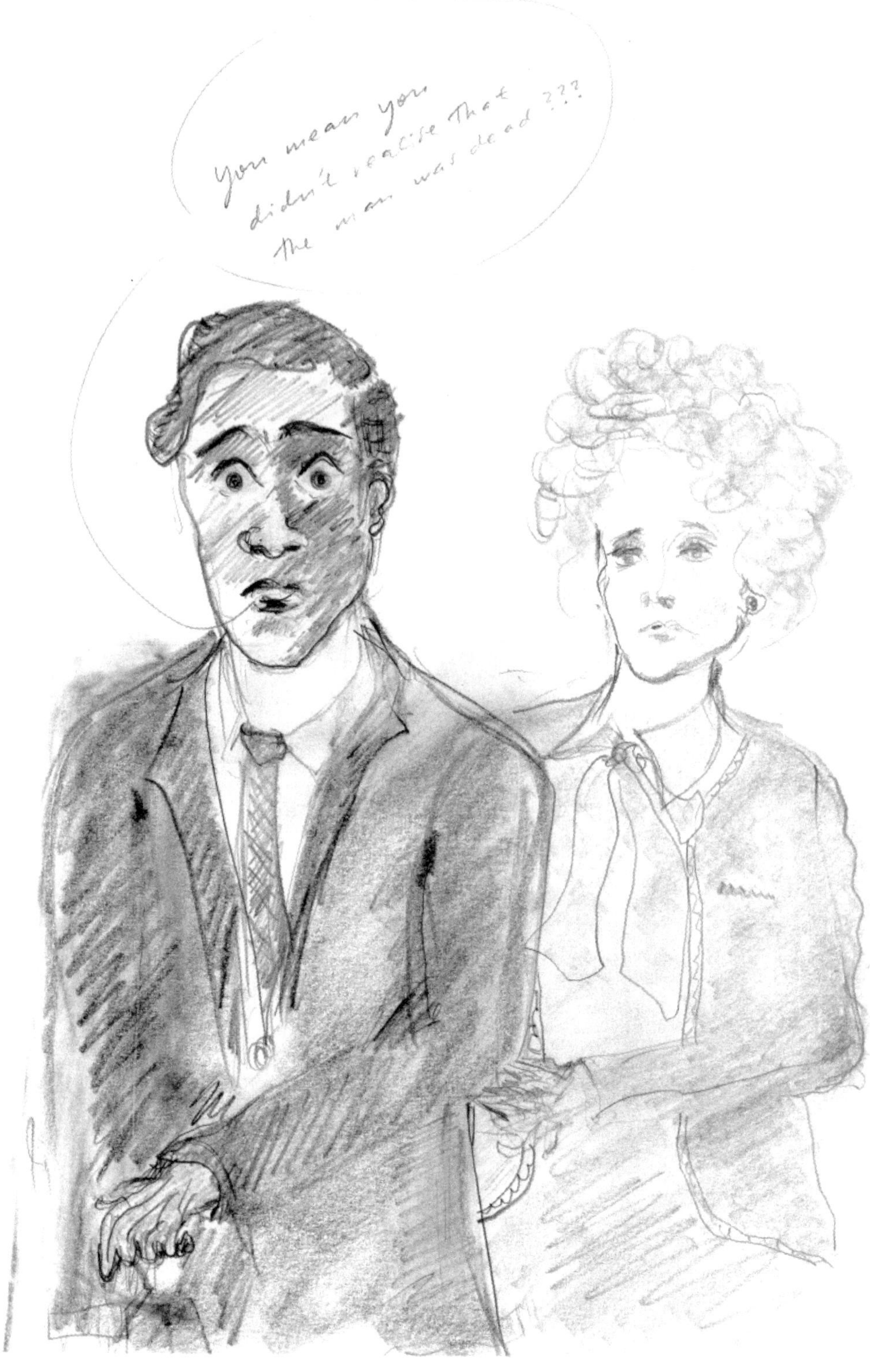
You mean you didn't realise that the man was dead???

Another military conflict ever-present in Basil's memory is the 1950–53 Korean war, in which he supposedly sustained a shrapnel wound in his leg. As we all know, it is when Basil finds himself in very difficult situations that he plays this last card. The only 'impartial' evidence adduced in the series to verify his actual participation in this war (twenty years before the series features him in the role of the hotel owner) is Sybil's remark to the young couple in The Wedding Party. Basil: "I fought in the Korean war, you know. I killed four men …" (he leaves huffily). Sybil: "He was in the catering corps. He poisoned them." There is no way of telling which, if either, of these comments has any truth in it. It might well be that to impress Sybil at a time when they were still in love, Basil explained a scar on his knee by saying that it was a Korean war wound. At the time Sybil was inclined to believe him, and it is a strange fact that she never suspects him of fraud when he starts his knee routine. For Basil it has remained a last resort, although he never set foot on the Korean peninsula, least of all in a war.

On the other hand, a roll-call of historical battlefields is featured in The Anniversary. Sybil, deeply hurt by what she believes to be Basil's forgetfulness of their wedding anniversary, asks him whether the date April 17 stirs any memories. Basil: "Anniversary of the battle of Agincourt? Trafalgar? Crécy? Poitiers? Yom Kippur?"

Let us take a brief look at these allusions, and see what the battles mentioned signified.

At Agincourt, in the present-day French *departement* of Pas-de-Calais, English soldiers under the command of Henry V won a triumphant victory in 1415 against the French army under d'Albret.

At Crécy-en-Ponthieu, the splendid and knightly French army, commanded by Philip VI, was defeated by an English peasant army reinforced with 'them yeomen bowmen' in 1346. The outcome of this battle struck a powerful blow at the continental feudal system.

At Cape Trafalgar, on the southern Spanish Atlantic coast, Lord

Nelson in 1805 secured Britain's dominion over the seas by breaking through the battle-line of the Spanish-French fleet, defeating it utterly.

At Poitiers, the Moors (Arabs), who had conquered the entire Iberian peninsula and much of France, were defeated and prevented from expanding farther north into Europe by the Frankish troops in the year 732.

Yom Kippur is not primarily a battlefield, nor a famous king or general. It is first and foremost the name of the celebration held on the Jewish day of atonement. However, in 1973 a skirmish between Israelis and Arabs escalated into a war situation, known in history books as the October War, but also nicknamed Yom Kippur. Basil is in all likelihood referring to this.

Battlefields are not the only historical references. In The Builders, Basil gets an unexpected call from O'Reilly. Upon Sybil's return to the hotel desk, where he's making the call, he does his best to conceal the real content of their conversation. Basil: "Oh, good, that'll be nice, won't it? I mean, we've waited for that wall about as long as Hadrian. No, Hadrian. The Emperor Hadrian – oh, it doesn't matter, I'll explain it next week. Goodbye."

What Basil is referring to is the 73-mile-long wall, with its numerous fortifications, that the Roman Emperor Hadrian built in 122-126 AD. The wall ran between present-day Bowness and Wallsend, and was designed not so much as a defensive bulwark against the Scottish tribes, whom the Romans considered impossible to civilise, but more as a base for northern army patrols. There may be an obscure point (coincidence) here, in that the ape-like Johnson's mother is coming down by train from Newcastle (the major northern city, near the wall, on the east coast) to visit grandchildren in Torquay (The Psychiatrist).

In Communication Problems, Basil tries to rid himself of Mrs. Richards as she urges him, once again, to call the police. In order to explain why he hasn't managed to get hold of them, he sarcastically throws in "They're very busy today ... there was a lot of blood shed at the Nell Gwynn tea-rooms last night." Apart from the obvious fact that a public tea-room in Torquay is perhaps the most unlikely crime scene one could possibly imagine, the name of the establishment nevertheless hides an allusion to a somewhat candid chapter in English history, shrouded not so much in legend as in pure gossip. Nell Gwynn (1650-1687) was an actress, more notorious for her beauty and coarse wit than for her acting talent. In astonishingly short time she worked herself up from being an orange seller at the Royal Theatre to become the favourite mistress of King Charles II, hence her nickname, Lady of the Bedchamber. She even bore the king a son, Charles Beauclerk, Duke of Saint Albans. It is obvious that Basil, by mentioning her name in connection with a (perhaps imaginary) tea-room, sees an obvious link between her reputation and the kind of 'light' conversation likely to be entertained in such a place.

In the same episode, Basil, still hopeful about the money he has just won on the horse, gets into an unusually happy mood. Before rubbing his hands singing: "The Camptown ladies sing this song, doo-daa, doo-daa, the Camptown race track five miles long, doo-daa, doo-daa-day ...," he prepares a snack for himself while simultaneously asking the chef: "Do you like *Cavalleria Rusticana*, Terry?" Terry: "I never had it, Mr. Fawlty."

The Italian composer Pietro Mascagni (1863-1945) wrote countless operas, but only one of them is still regularly staged and universally hailed as a masterpiece, *Cavalleria Rusticana*. A famous Intermezzo from this one-act opera is often played separately and in a multitude of arrangements. Terry's answer clearly reveals that he has no idea what Basil is referring to. He thinks it's like paëlla ...

Speaking of music, it should be mentioned that the melody introducing each episode was composed by a certain Dennis Wil-

139

son and arranged for string quartet by Byron Olson (not the lord this time either!). Other musical themes featured in the series include the opening bars of Johannes Brahms' third symphony (A Touch of Class), Pjotr Tchaikowsky's Dance of the Sugar Plum Fairy from The Nutcracker Suite (The Builders), and a fragment of one of Chopin's Ballades (The Wedding Party).

Throughout the episode Communication Problems, the old tale of S:t George and the Dragon plays a prominent part. As we all know, one of Basil's favourite nicknames for his wife is 'the old dragon,' so we might infer that he sees himself as a dragon-slayer of sorts.

The tale of S:t George and the Dragon was first recorded in a collection of medieval anecdotes called *Legenda Aurea* (The Golden Legend). Silene, so the story goes, was a town set beside a lake in Lydia (today's western Turkey), which had been besieged by a fire-breathing dragon who lived in the lake. The dragon threatened to destroy the town unless the citizens paid him tribute in the form of young maidens, whom he devoured. There came a day when the king's daughter was chosen by lot as the next victim. As she waited for the dragon to rise from the water and devour her, a noble knight appeared. He slew the dragon and thus delivered the town from evil. He eventually became a saint through his martyrdom at the hands of the Romans, who accused him of trying to convert the citizens of Silene to the despised Christian faith.

The reverberations of this piece of hagiography are far-reaching in Fawlty Towers. For instance, the noble mare so close to carrying S:t Basil to glory was called, as we have noted above, Dragonfly …

And since we are now grazing the vast field of legendary and literary allusions, what could be better than to offer this famous quote from Hamlet's soliloquy as presented by Basil Fawlty. Basil: (to the *three* doctors Abbott in The Psychiatrist) "Fine. Well … I'll leave you to it, then. I mean, to go to bed – to sleep, perchance to dream … ("To sleep, perchance to dream – ay, there's the rub." Shakespeare's *Hamlet*, Act III, Scene I).

To conclude our examination of these instances of Basil's erudition, I would like to draw the reader's attention to two references from the contemporary literary scene. Harold Robbins is avowedly a great favourite of both Sybil and the Hamiltons (Waldorf Salad). Mr. Hamilton: (to Basil) "We both like him." Basil: "Oh, Harold Robbins, I thought you meant Harold Robinson …"

Sybil's admiration of this same author is expressed with particular eloquence. "His men are all so interesting. Ruthless and sexy and … powerful." It seems almost unnecessary to note that Harold Robbins is an enormously successful best-selling writer, whose compellingly banal books, such as *The Secret, The Pirate, Never Leave Me* and (the evergreen classic featured in Waldorf Salad), *Never Love a Stranger*, still attract a huge readership and top sales lists all over the world.

Last, but not least, there is the famous bedroom episode, the horrors of which have already been described, but are so crucial that they bear repetition. Sybil and Basil are shown in their respective beds, Sybil, hair in curlers, shrouded in a purple négligée, reading a comic strip, eating chocolates, taking the cherries out of her mouth and leaving them in the ashtray, smoking a cigarette, laughing as she inhales and talks to Audrey at the same time. Basil, nauseated, tries to cover his ears while concentrating on the copy of *Jaws* in his lap. The cover shows the gigantic shark with its rows of razor-sharp teeth, ready and eager to attack, and to kill …

# 5

# THE OCCULT
# FAWLTY TOWERS

THE WORDS 'FAWLTY' AND 'Towers' each have 6 letters, making a total of 12. Not only are there 12 episodes of the show, but they are also divided into two series, each containing 6 episodes. The number 12 is symbolically related, among other things, to the 12 zodiacal signs, to the 12 seats around King Arthur's round table, as well as to the 12 disciples – Jesus himself being represented by the number 13. In symbolic terms therefore the number 12 represents completeness, an event come full circle.

As the number 13 symbolises Christ himself, we should consequently attach deep symbolical significance to the thirteenth, never televised episode, The Robbers, the text of which has been reproduced in its entirety at the end of this book. In this concluding episode, Basil performs a Kierkegaardian leap of faith. It is the ultimate sacrifice, beyond mere morality and ethics, a counterpart to the scriptural story of Abraham's obedience to God's will that he sacrifice his son Isaac. Basil acts in relation to a similar calling from the Unknown, and in this episode, his destiny is at last made manifest. By insisting upon the uniqueness of his action, Basil here assumes the role of the eternal redeemer who sacrifices his soul and conscience in order to be able to live on in another world.

According to Sybil, in A Touch of Class, not the sky, but 22 rooms is the limit. It is almost uncanny that the number 22 corresponds to the number of trump cards in the mystical tarot deck. These 22 Major Arcana cards are usually interpreted as archetypes, governing and shaping human perception of the spiritual and psychic worlds. The series of the Major Arcana cards actually ends with card number 21, The Universe, but there is also a number zero called The Fool, and so there are, in spite of their odd numbering, 22 in all. We shall return to the significance of this at the end of this chapter.

Numerology is the occult science which posits that a combination of specific numbers is at the root of divine creation. This idea has especially pervaded Jewish mysticism, expressed in the Kabbalah, in which the tree of life is represented as an interplay between abstract principles that can also be defined as symbolically significant relationships between numbers. A typical procedure to determine the symbolical meaning of, say, a compound number, would be to break it down into single numbers. Thus, if we add the number of rooms, 22, to the number of episodes, 12, we get 34, and if we break that number down to 3 and 4 and add the terms we get 7, which is the number of the room assigned to the righteous angel in disguise – the cockney police inspector Danny – who arrives at the hotel immediately after Sybil has pronounced her verdict on the limits of their universe, "Number 7 is free, Basil."

The numbers 7 and 22 can also be seen to have a significant relation to the menorah of the Hebrews: the seven-armed candlestick whose form was specified by God to Moses on Mount Sinai. Made of solid gold, to represent the unity of the divine world of emanations, it revolves around its axis of grace, has right and left arms signifying mercy and severity, $10+1$ sefirotic positions and 22 decorations ($10+1=11$; $11+11=22$). Without going further into the interaction of the primordial spiritual principles summed up in the word Sephirots, we can nevertheless conclude that this coincidence – if indeed there's such a thing as chance! – of symbolically significant numbers is striking.

The number of recurring characters in the show is also 7. There are two ways of counting here. Either one counts Miss Tibbs and Miss Gatsby as one, since they always, Gemini-like, appear together (exception made for The Kipper and the Corpse), or one counts them separately as two and leaves chef Terry out. (He doesn't appear in the first six shows, although he might be suspected of lurking unseen somewhere in the kitchen.) Frequent reference is made to him in the first six shows. For example, Hutchison, in The Hotel Inspectors: "… in a case like this where the order has been changed and the chef's been informed, it is obviously his responsibility." I myself prefer this method of counting, and like to assume that Terry was there all the time, though he wasn't seen by us. To regard the Ladies as one entity seems feasible to me.

The number 7 may also be seen in correlation to the 7 celestial spheres supporting the planetary bodies visible to the naked eye, which provided the basis for the old geocentric cosmology. In this system a total number of 7 moving heavenly bodies (Moon, Mercury, Venus, Mars, Jupiter, Saturn and Sun) were considered as each orbiting its own sphere, and corresponding to specific symbolic qualities. These characteristics were interpreted in dramatic terms; in fact they were seen as interacting agents having human characteristics. Their effect on human life was carefully studied and prognosticated in 'sciences' such as astrology, hermeticism, alchemy and tarot. In other words, we have here 7 regular characters – as opposed to the random coming and going of other characters – moving through the 12 episodes as if they were in reality 7 heavenly bodies orbiting the zodiac. The other actors in the Towers episodes may by analogy be regarded as comets, meteorites and other unpredictable phenomena capable of disturbing the workings of a 'perfect' enclosed planetary system.

In hermetic systems the 7 planets are also related to 7 metals supposed to correspond to certain character traits. The Sun is gold; the Moon is silver; Mercury quicksilver; Venus copper; Jupiter pewter and Saturn lead. The 7 planets are also considered rulers of the signs of the zodiac. It follows that the majority of these bodies rule more than one zodiacal sign. (It should be mentioned here that the traditional way of interpreting the signs in relation to 7 governing planets has now been superseded by a system in which the new planets discovered by telescope in the scientific era – Neptune, Uranus and Pluto – are each accorded one zodiacal sign.) The Sun and the Moon obviously correspond to the married couple at the centre of the action. The Major, the military man, is Mars. The radiant Polly is Venus. The Ladies are Mercury (related to the astrological sign of Gemini), the jovial Terry is Jupiter, and the devil himself, Manuel, is Saturn.

Symbolically significant in this respect is that Andrew Sachs, the actor who plays Manuel, is of Jewish descent. Hermetic tradition – based on the Gnostic interpretation of Yahweh (the letters 'y,' 'a' and 'w' are actually part of the word Fawlty!) as the evil principle, the so-called demiurge of the universe – maintains that the primordial god Saturn, begetter of the golden age associated with the myth of the sunken Atlantis and paradise on earth among the ancient Greeks, is the dark principle of this world, opposed to the father of light. It is consequential that Andrew Sachs, as Manuel, should have to endure suffering and humiliation in this world, both because he is a Jew and because he is the offspring of the dark and fearsome Saturn (Yahweh). That Manuel is necessarily the scapegoat, not to say the sacrificial lamb, of the series, reveals itself in his very name. Manuel is Spanish for Immanuel, another name for Jesus Christ himself.

The names Basil and Sybil have far-reaching connotations too. In ancient Greek, *basileus* was the word for king and a *sybil* was an oracle who induced trances used either to prophesy to the people and their leaders, or incite them to action.[18]

Symbolically then, the fight between Basil and Sybil is the fight between the temporal power of the king and the *nemesis divina* (divine revenge) embodied in the sybilline oracle. Manuel is the sacrificial victim, and it should come as no surprise to us that Manuel and Sybil hardly ever interact during the entire 12 episodes – she is willing to accept any sacrifice made to her.

In the previous chapter we have demonstrated that an essential attribute of Fawlty Towers is verbal misunderstanding leading to a breakdown of communication. Now, what myth does that remind us of? But, of course, the Tower of Babel! The Tower is already present in the hotel's name, and the myth perfectly corresponds to the everyday reality of its denizens.

In the first episode Basil hubristically exclaims, "The sky's the limit." (Indeed, the reason for building the Babylonian edifice was to reach all the way to heaven.) The sybil, Basil's Sybil, warns him of his human limitations, but he must continue to pursue his goal. At this point the supreme being, Yahweh, brings about the confusion of tongues. Communication between the builders (see the episode of the same name) thereafter ceases, and the blame for it all is put on the Jews, personified here by Manuel.

The confusion of tongues leads to a communication problem which proves that the Tower is in truth Fawlty. The hotel sign in this key episode (Communication Problems) specifically shows that there is but one tower here (Fawlty Tower), not a plurality, which again brings to mind the symbolism of the Major Arcana in the tarot. The Tower is trump-card number 16 – and 16, Elmwood

---

[18] Another name sometimes used for this kind of soothsayer and sorceress is a Python …

Avenue, is the address of the hotel (see Polly's conversation with the deliveryman, Kerr, in The Builders) – presaging imminent destruction, or, in internalised psychological terms: the shattering of the ego. And if this were not already striking enough, the ominous Mrs. Richards has been given room 22, which, as we already know, represents 'the sky', 'the limit'. Number 22 is also the tarot trump corresponding to trump number zero, The Fool, since it follows the nominal last card, number 21, The Universe, in the Major Arcana.

So, if we accept the idea proposed earlier that the Basilean universe coincides with a Gnostic conception of the world, it follows that The Universe in question is the artefact of a demiurge, in other words, of a creative but far-from-perfect agent who has fashioned the world according to his own lights. The Gnostic idea of the work of the demiurge – significantly derived from the Greek word *démios*, meaning 'of the people' – was this, that an imperfect God must by definition be unable to create a perfect world. This would have been fair enough if God hadn't, by way of the Scriptures, proclaimed that he was not only the one true God, but also an arbitrarily intolerant, jealous, and punitive tyrant!

The Gnostics eventually turned their backs on this presumptuous divinity 'for the people,' an act for which they were ruthlessly persecuted by the Roman Catholic Church. Nevertheless, they insisted that it is possible to achieve freedom of the mind, and that the godhead resides within us in the form of a divine spark, making the illumined individual perfect, no matter what his actions seem to be, or to mean, to the world around him.

Seen in this light, Basil's attempt to defeat Mrs. Richards represents, on the one hand, his struggle against the demiurge (his wife, other women, all imaginable guests, his station in life and a host of other circumstances keeping him shackled and tied to earth) and, on the other, against the shattering of his ego. This paves the way

for the leap of faith that only The Fool, number zero, the innocent human being, can make.

Thus, the mythical ramifications of the series are as undeniable as are its inherent mysticism and Kabbalistic play on words. Of special interest in the numerological aspect are the names of the undertakers in The Kipper and the Corpse: Mr. Xerxes, Miss Young and Mr. Zebedee. The letters X, Y and Z, on which their names have been based, are common in mathematics where they denote unknown or unspecified factors. I shall leave these to the readers' imagination, and hint only that the alphabetical symbols are obviously connected with death and the mysterious encounter with an unknown Boss …

In the matter of Jewish mysticism, there is also the extraordinary symbolism hidden in the emblem on the covers of the menus on the infamous Gourmet Night. For some reason, a long, drawn-out argument (if 'yes, she can,' 'no, she can't,' 'yes, she can,' 'no, she can't,' may be considered as such) is carried on between Basil and

Sybil in regard to Polly's ability to design the menu. Since Sybil on this occasion supports Polly, she naturally gets her own way, and the menu cards are eventually drawn by Polly. Polly even asks Basil if he likes them, and he curtly says, "No."

Well, that's the end of that, but the viewer has a few seconds to see how she actually designed the card, and what she drew on the front cover, namely an abstract picture of two towers, one black and the other white. In Jewish and Masonic symbolism the black and white pillars/towers are known by the names of Boas and Yachin, originally two copper pillars in Solomon's temple in Jerusalem. In Jewish mysticism they are interpreted as being the pillars of Mercy and Severity (Love and Law). Like the concepts of yin and yang they are by extension symbolically linked to other dual phenomena such as day and night, dry and moist, male and female.

Although the representation of the two towers is, as I have said, rather in the abstract, there can be no doubt that the designer must have had the eternal antagonism of the black and white pieces of the chess-board in mind. In A. E. Waite's tarot deck the white pillar with the black initial 'J' and the black pillar with the white initial 'B' are depicted in the Major Arcana card number 2, The High Priestess. The two towers represent the antagonists, wholly unreconcileable forces – in this case, man and woman.

Masonic symbolism played a prominent role in some of the Monty Python sketches written by John Cleese and Graham Chapman. Quite remarkable is the one in which an architect (Cleese) has been invited to present, before an audience of distinguished gentlemen, a prospective model of a block of flats. He goes on to explain how the tenants themselves are carried along conveyor belts only to be slaughtered by rotating knives protruding from the walls ... Cleese pretends to be very much surprised when this device, in his view genial, does not turn out to be exactly what the customer had in mind. He soon changes his attitude to one of absolute servility, claiming that the only thing that really matters to him is to be allowed membership in the same golf club as the distinguished members of the commission. When politely rejected for the tenth time, he begins spitting venom over them, suggesting they stick their golf clubs up certain places and ridiculing their special Masonic handshakes. At the end of the sketch, Cleese has finally been driven out of the room, and the gentlemen in their dinner jackets are actually seen performing some elaborate ceremony of departure, involving mysterious handshakes and other secret signs.

It is well known that Masonic symbolism not only draws on the mystical circumstances surrounding the legendary construction of Solomon's temple in Jerusalem, but also on the medieval tradition of allowing master masons to travel from one cathedral building site to another without having to provide for their own subsistence. The handshakes were part of an identification system by which an unknown mason could introduce himself to another master mason, and in this way prove that he belonged to the same guild and fraternity as the latter. Considering how often the erection of twin towers came to meet a master builder's idea of architectural balance, it is not surprising to see how the Fawlty Twin Towers, unconsciously as it were, aspire to a similar mysterious perfection and – as recent events on lower Manhattan have shown – to a similarly apocalyptic end as well.

# 6

# HOW IT ALL
# CAME ABOUT

# SOME NOTES ON THE
# HISTORICAL BACKGROUND

IF EVER THERE WAS a specific moment in time when Fawlty Towers was conceived, it may very well have been on May 12, 1971. This was the legendary date when the Monty Python cast and crew on location in the Torquay area, checked in at the apparently attractive, modern hotel Gleneagles in Torquay (the name of which was to furtively recur in the Fawlty Towers episode The Builders, where Basil has occasion to tell the Ladies that, "you have to go to Gleneagles for your din-dins tonight.").

In most hagiographic literature pertaining to S:t John, the events following their arrival at Gleneagles have been related in pious detail. However, for the benefit of those readers who, in spite of the solid documentation now existing on the subject, still happen to be unfamilar with these crucial events, I shall allow for a short recapitulation.[19]

The owners of the hotel Gleneagles were a Mr. and Mrs. Donald Sinclair. By a singular twist of fate, these two good people were predestined to become the prototypes of the legendary Basil and Sybil Fawlty, thus unwittingly the avatars of legend.[20]

Apparently a wilful man, Donald Sinclair did not hesitate to impose his whims and convictions on others. Without the 'slightest' provocation he vociferously began complaining about the behaviour of his guests. He is said to have suspected Eric Idle of secreting a bomb in his bag, and to have made pejorative remarks on Terry Gilliam's American (read: uncivilised) way of wielding his knife and fork. When, in addition, it proved impossible to get a drink on the premises, the Monty Python crew decided to de-camp and find a hotel more conducive to conviviality. They all promptly left, with the exception, that is, of John Cleese, who had a strange premonition. He felt that he had to stay and dig deeper into, perhaps even make a bet on a mining concession in this mother lode of golden eccentricity. Connie Booth joined him at the hotel. A solemn vow was made to create something of note out of this encounter with a living phenomenon. The promise became overwhelming reality and even survived the official collapse of their marriage in 1978. In 1979 a second set of six episodes featuring the same cast was broadcast by the BBC.

However, the now so famous series was not entirely unprece-dented. On May 31, 1971 the episode No Ill Feeling in the television

---

19 As far as the general information above is concerned, I should point out that some of it can be found on various Internet sites. However, most of the Fawlty Towers-related mate-rial presented on the Net seems to draw principally on Jonathan Margolis' 1991 biography, *Cleese Encounters* (the eighth chapter of the book deals with the time period in which John Cleese wrote and produced Fawlty Towers together with Connie Booth). The facts gathered and the theories propounded in Margolis' biography are in turn based on numerous media interviews with John Cleese, and on the many newspaper/periodical articles that the sub-ject matter and its creators have generated over time. Another principal and thoroughly up-dated source of information is the recently published, as well as earlier mentioned, *Fawlty Towers Fully Booked* by Morris Bright and Robert Ross, which contains lots of valuable background information as well as relevant interview material. I acknowledge my gratitude to all.

20 At the time of writing, Mr. Sinclair, according to the testimony of his wife, has been peacefully dead for many years, although Mrs. Sinclair still feels haunted by the spectre of caricature. Recently she publicly declared that she is intent on suing the authors for a large sum of money in recompense for the disrepute their series brought her once respectable establishment. "Of course, I was running the place," Mrs. Sinclair candidly replied when asked if there were any similarities whatsoever between her deceased husband and the fictio-nal character of Basil Fawlty, "but he wasn't as bad as they made him out to be."

comedy series *Doctor at Large* was aired, the script written by John Cleese. The scenario and the characters were in many ways rough prototypes of the ones later developed and refined in Fawlty Towers. There was, apart from the main character, Dr. Upton, a gimcrack hotel, a capricious and irritable hotel owner, an overbearing bore, and an array of elderly ladies. Producer Humphrey Barclay felt that the episode contained within it the seed of a whole series, but John Cleese did not agree at the time. So the idea was to lie dormant until the day Cleese decided to leave the Monty Python group to its own devices. Eager to work more closely with his wife on a writing project, opportunity knocked on their door when Jimmy Gilbert, head of light entertainment at BBC, commissioned them to write a 20-minute pilot episode about anything they fancied. Searching their memories they again saw Mr. Sinclair rear his ominous head over the roofs and pinnacles of Torquay. Soon the silhouette of the Towers themselves began to loom in the background.

The twelve episodes of Fawlty Towers were subsequently written and filmed in two different time periods – an interval of almost five years separating them. But in spite of this extended interlude, the series came to reveal an extraordinary homogeneity that exists parallel to its advancing development from A Touch of Class, which was the first to be televised on September 19, 1974, to Basil the Rat, the last, which was aired October 25, 1979 (it was supposed to be televised that spring, but union action – to Cleese's immense joy – resulted in its postponement).

In some instances the recording sessions were just as full of drama as the action they were supposed to depict. A famous anecdote relates that Andrew Sachs in connection with the shooting of The Wedding Party, received such a nasty blow on his head from the frying-pan wielded by Basil, that he was "left woozy for two days." (It has not been revealed if Cleese ever made reparation to his long-suffering deuteragonist, for instance by sending him flo-

wers, or even a bottle of whisky adorned with a card saying: "Cheer up, for God's sake!")

Later, during the shooting of the first series, Sachs was going to see more misfortune come his way. In The Germans, his role figure Manuel was supposed to set himself on fire when meddling with the kitchen stove. Andrew Sachs' dedication to the task was such that he burnt himself badly and sustained severe scarring to his shoulder. Set against the total fee of £450 Sachs is said to have received for his work throughout the entire series, the £700 he was granted in compensation for his injuries represents a sizeable award.

Relevant sources are not quite unanimous on this point, but general consensus seems to have accepted as credible the proposition that each episode had to go through about ten drafts and four months of work before being presented to the viewing public.

What about the financial reward then? Well, what Connie

Booth initially got out of it, I have been unable to find out. John Cleese on the other hand has candidly confessed in an interview that he received £1,000 for the first series of six episodes in 1975, and £9,000 for the second in 1979. Considering the tremendous increase in popularity the show has known since that time, any reasonable percentage on its diffusion and distribution in the form of televised reruns, video cassettes, DVDs, printed scripts, records, etc., must amount to some quite astounding figure. However, in view of the insignificant amount of money initially set aside to finance production, we can probably rule out pecuniary gain as being of much interest to either John Cleese or Connie Booth. As is the case with all works of genuine inspiration, not to say of pure genius, the edifice of Fawlty Towers appears to have been erected 'for its own sake.'

# PRODUCTION, SETS AND COSTUME

THE GENERAL *mise en scene* of all Fawlty Towers episodes is invariably the same, the interior of the hotel comprising the same few rooms: lobby, dining-room, kitchen and lounge. In addition to this familiar environment there are a few exterior scenes as well. According to online and other sources, these outdoor scenes were all shot on location at a villa in the small village of Woburn Green, near High Wycombe, a town midway between London and Oxford, in Buckinghamshire. The villa itself was called the Woburn Grange Country Club in Bourn End. The British Location Guide states that it was later an Indian restaurant and then a nightclub, called 'Basil' of all things. The entire house was ravaged by fire some years ago and thereafter demolished. No vestige of its glorious past remains today, and there are eight new buildings on the site (there is a site on the Internet where one can see photos of how the area actually looks today).

There are a few scenes in which parts of the town itself form the backdrop: the street where André's restaurant is located as well as the street in which Basil is seen trashing the car (Gourmet Night). There is also an outdoor scene in A Touch of Class where we see Polly leave the bank and Mr. Brown watch Lord Melbury as he leaves the jeweller's shop. John Margolis (*Cleese Encounters*) states that the outdoor scene in which Basil is seen driving his car to Andrés restaurant was shot while the car was driven by Cleese down a main street near Acton. *Fawlty Towers Fully Booked* in turn certifies that André's restaurant itself was located at 294, Preston Road in Harrow, whereas the trashing-the-car scene in the same episode was filmed in Mentmore Close in Kenton, north London.

As for the one remaining town scene from A Touch of Class, I have been unable to find out where it was filmed. Since it is of course out of the question that a BBC film crew on a low-budget mission would have gone all the way down to the English Riviera for a few seconds worth of real Torquay ambience, we might confidently surmise that these images, like all the other outdoor scenes, were captured in some location close to London.

One thing is for sure, however. The lanky person who steps out of Joseph Lambert's jeweller's shop, and whom we are supposed to take for Lord Melbury, is not Michael Gwynn, who plays his lordship in the indoor scenes at the hotel. First of all, the chap in the street has no moustache. Secondly, he wears glasses – obviously with the intention of disguising himself while 'on business' in town. Even if this person had appeared with a moustache and without glasses, he still would have looked very different from the other Lord Melbury. His posture and body movements character-ise an altogether different person. In fact, this Lord Melbury is an impostor of the impostor – an illusion within the illusion which intensifies the metaphysical vertigo symptomatic of our percep-tion of the Towers.

There might be a practical reason for this apparent anomaly. Ac-cording to producer/director of the first Fawlty Towers series (as well as of the Monty Python shows from 1969 onward), John Howard Davies, all inserts were filmed weeks before the produc-tion of the actual shows and then painstakingly slotted in. Possibly Michael Gwynn was not available (or not even yet asked to play the role!) on the day when the outdoor scenes of the first episode were to be filmed. In other words, somebody had to impersonate him. Avoiding close-up photography of the 'stunt's' face, John Howard Davies thought he could get away with the deception. In the normal way of things he would have done, of course, but then he couldn't possibly have foreseen that while shooting the pilot episode of a new British sitcom, the entire team was about to make history, and put sleepy old Torquay on the world map.

Another and more important question is of course, "Where were the indoor scenes filmed?" The answer is: in the BBC studios. Although we, the spectators, are not supposed to notice this, we get more than subtle hints about it. For example, we never witness any actor enter the hotel frontally when the camera picks him or her up from within the lobby. They always enter and exit to and from the right, behind the wall next to the entrance. This door is always curiously open in the daytime, regardless of British weather conditions.

A further indication is that when doors are slammed, or Basil and Manuel are engaged in violent goings-on, we often see the walls wobble and visibly give way. This shows that at least some of them are really quite insubstantial – probably no more than mobile room-dividers (see, for example, The Builders). Upon closer scrutiny (see Basil's climbing the ladder "to see girl in room" in The Psychiatrist) the windows too turn out to be very frail. And they don't have the transparency of ordinary glass, but seem to be made of plastic.

In addition, the outdoor scenery, as viewed through the main entrance from the lobby, is in all episodes projected on to screens on which the background vegetation continually changes. The same screens also provide exterior background through the windows of the bar and dining-room. The sea "in between the land and the sky" is a projection of this kind as well. We may also notice that although these screens always present exteriors of lush vegetation (in summer time), most of the outdoor scenes have obviously been shot during winter, as there are no leaves on the bigger trees, and it is cold and damp.

Neither do we ever see any of the walls or windows on the side of the lobby facing the entrance, or of the dining-room wall opposite the kitchen, or of the wall in the bar opposite the one facing the car park and the garden. On this showing we may safely conclude that the staircase leading to the upper rooms was no more than another means of entry and exit for the actors, since, in reality, the studio set featured seven separate movable 'rooms', each one of which must have been like a traditional theatre facing the spectator on one of its four sides. This vector must have been open to accommodate crew, sound equipment and cameras. Thus, the set, as we see it, most likely coincided with the director's line of vision, probably identical with that of the live audience as well.

The audience, yes. The twelve episodes were actually recorded in marathon Sunday sessions, beginning with camera rehearsals in the morning – by then the ensemble had already rehearsed without cameras for a week. By 4:00 on the Sunday afternoon it was time for dress rehearsal and the recordings with the live audience were usually not finished until around 10:00 p.m. Each episode required the incredible number of four hundred different camera shots, meaning that there was on average a cut every fourth second, "Almost double compared to other BBC shows, and enough to make American actors grow pale," according to John Cleese (*Cleese Encounters*). In other words, the procedures leading up to the finished product – even if we leave out the elaborate plotting, writing and rewriting of each episode – were much more complicated and drawn out than for any other British sitcom of that time. Who knows, maybe Fawlty Towers still holds the record on camera angles for any situation comedy in the world?

After this brief résumé of the technical aspects of the production, let us now turn our attention to the interior décor. We should then first of all bear in mind that the chronological sequence in which the episodes of the two series were shown – beginning with A Touch of Class, followed by The Builders etc. – does not necessarily reflect the order in which they were produced. The fire alarm, for instance, gives us a clue. Conspicuous by its absence in the first four episodes, it is first seen in Gourmet Night (the fifth episode to be shown) although it has no part in the action here. Conversely, in the sixth and last episode of the first series, The Germans, the alarm bell does indeed play a very essential role. So, although broadcast first, Gourmet Night was in all likelihood filmed after The Germans, since it would have made absolutely no sense to introduce an alarm bell on stage without putting it to any use.

The kitchen door installed in the second episode (The Builders) is paradoxically already in place in the first episode (A Touch of Class). However in this opening episode it is located much further to the right, thus allowing a dark wooden bench to fit into the space between the door and the staircase. In later episodes this space has disappeared, and the wooden bench is consequently placed to the right of the door (see for example The Wedding Party, number three, and The Hotel Inspectors, number four). At the beginning of The Builders (number two), there is no kitchen door at all, and the door to the left of the main entrance is still there. This door is in place in A Touch of Class too. It is only after The Builders that it disappears altogether – all rather confusing!

Still, in spite of there being a kitchen door in A Touch of Class and none at the beginning of The Builders, there are good reasons to believe that the former really was the first episode to be filmed. One piece of evidence in support of this is that the hotel sign (shown at the beginning of all but one episode, The Germans, to the accompaniment of the string quartet playing the Fawlty Towers theme) is virtually intact, the only anomaly being a final sagging 'S.'

In most of the following episodes the sign has been exposed to some more or less obscene word-play. Sometimes there is just one letter missing; in The Psychiatrist we catch a glimpse of the mischievous boy responsible for the mutilations. A list of the semiotic mutations of the hotel sign is given below in the order of appearance.

A Touch of Class: FAWLTY TOWERS (with sagging S)
The Builders: FAWLTY TOWER (with sagging L)
The Wedding Party: FARTY TOWER (with sagging W)
The Hotel Inspectors: FAW TY TO WER
Gourmet Night: WARTY TOWELS
The Germans: (Sign not shown)
Communication Problems: FAWLTY TOWER (with sagging L)
The Psychiatrist: WATERY FOWLS (with boy seen manipulating the letters)
Waldorf Salad: FLAY OTTERS
The Kipper and the Corpse: FATTY OWLS
The Anniversary: FLOWERY TWATS
Basil the Rat: FARTY TOWELS

As we can see, the correct spelling of the hotel name appears only once – in A Touch of Class. We may infer from this that it was the first episode to be filmed, and there are other indications that such was the case. The quality of the colour reproduction is conspicuously poor. This is the only episode in which the wallpaper in the lobby appears to be light green and the floor red. In all other episodes the first is as yellow as ripe wheat, and the other a dark-bluish green. There is actually a brownish tinge to all the colours in this episode, a defect that is absent in the following shows. A Touch of Class is also the only episode that features a rack of postcards at the far end of the lobby desk.

The picture of the ship above the door (blocked off in The Builders) is not the same as in that episode either. In the former it looks like a brig, in the latter like a clipper. One last detail. When Danny Brown addresses Basil as "waiter", the latter turns and in so doing lets us see the face of Miss Tibbs. I have stopped my video recorder here and, shot by shot, scrutinised the image of the lady. My conclusion is that it may very well be Miss Tibbs, but I can swear that the actress playing her is not Gilly Flower. It must be an impostor – another one!

The brown and somewhat patinated tinge mentioned above has largely disappeared in The Builders. Also missing in subsequent episodes is the sideboard with breakfast china to the left of the swinging doors that lead to the kitchen. The lighting has been enhanced, and it really seems as if the quest for a better class of clientele (the *raison d'être* of the first episode) had made the hotel residents aware of the fact that they must conform to a certain standard. A noticeable 'touch of class' has been brought to the scenario by the con-artist Lord Melbury. From then onward all uncertainties are gone. The ship has been launched; it has left the muddy waters of the harbour and embarked on its epic voyage over seas of laughter.


The hotel's interior décor thus keeps changing a little from one episode to the next. But after the two first shows such variation is very slight within each set of six shows. Considering that a near five-year gap separates the first from the second series, it is not surprising that observable changes would occur between The Germans (number six in the first series) and Communication Problems (number one in the second series).

And here's the surprise: probably not one single piece of furniture from the first series survives into the second. The reason why we do not at once notice this is that each piece has been replaced by very carefully chosen similar items. (That the grandfather clock, exceptionally, had to be moved to the side of the entrance hall in The Germans is readily explained: there had to be room for Basil's stage business with the moose's head). The antique grandfather clock in the second series is not the same as the clock in the first, the 'antlers' of the former being much more pointed, actually veritable devil's horns! The barometer of the first series is more elaborately carved than its successor. The banker's desk in the office is black in the first series, brown and bigger in the second. The lacquered wooden glass cabinet in the hallway leading to the lounge is not the same. The chairs and the tables in the lounges are different, as is the slot machine. Similar changes can be observed in the dining-room and in the lobby, where chairs and tables have changed places.[21]

Although the studio set may well have been preserved for possible future use, original items of furniture – probably not BBC property in the first place, but hired – could not perhaps be located after an interval of five years, and were replaced by pieces as apparently identical as possible. And the set decorator did a very good job. It takes an attentive eye to see that such a conspicuous piece as the grandfather clock isn't the same one in all episodes, and the eye of a true fanatic to discern that the little wooden bench between the kitchen door and the dining room has been changed as well.

On the other hand, the lavish flower arrangements are notably variable. It is at first hard to imagine that any one in the hotbed of

---

[21] Basil's collection of imperial coins seems to have made its one and only appearance in A Touch of Class.

the Towers would care that much for flowers, but their abundance, in as many beautiful vases, is testimony that such a person really exists. Is it Polly? In terms of decoration, Sybil is decidedly more interested in her hair, and Basil couldn't care less, probably preferring the ease of maintenance of plastic flowers. So, unless we were to suspect Terry or Manuel of having a secret passion for sumptous flower arrangements, they must be of Polly's doing.

Speaking of sumptuousness, there should be a word here about the quantity of colourful ties featured throughout the series. The Major is a case in point, always dressed in elegant suits and becoming ties. Basil is mostly seen in a suit and tie, sometimes just in cardigan and cravat though. His most winning confection, however, is the check jacket with green chest panels, which he dons for what turns out to be an after all not so enjoyable weekend of golf with Sybil – "It's called style dear. You would never understand" (The Builders). Otherwise, Basil's style of dress is remarkably conservative – colours range from brown to grey, and there may occasionally be a dark green cardigan as well. Apart from the check jacket, there is never an attempt at extravagance on his part.

Sybil's wardrobe and hairstyles, on the other hand, would indeed merit a chapter to themselves. In this context we shall have to limit ourselves to a general description. The most immediately striking visible feature of Sybil is, as any spectator can easily verify, her remarkable predilection for bouffant wigs and knotted scarves – sometimes even enhanced with Nottingham lace. Early on in A Touch of Class she sets the tone by throwing a violet jacket over her white blouse with its generously flowing flouncy bow, only to subsequently leave the hotel wearing a leopard-skin coat. It is noteworthy that she (exception made for the opening of The Wedding Party) never wears a dress but always a combination of skirt and blouse. If she wears a jacket, it is generally of the same colour and design as that of the skirt. The colours of her dress (except in the above-mentioned A Touch of Class) range from deep blue, violet and purple to piggy-pink – ardent admirers of Queen Elizabeth's impeccable taste and flare for stylish colour combinations might already have noticed that Sybil's clothes sometimes actually aspire to royal splendour. And what a match it makes with her tremendous syllabub-like dyed hair! As the series progresses, Sybil's wigs have a general tendency to get fluffier and fluffier, and Basil's reference to a rat's maze does not seem entirely unjustified. What does she keep in there? The secret is well guarded. It is quite possible that not even Basil has ever seen her hair in its natural state – perhaps she's bald?

Polly's clothes range from the modestly elegant to the transparently sexy. In the first episode she has been assigned a purely domestic role and her dress is consequently unsensational. Notwithstanding the necessity of attuning Polly's clothing to the general ambiance of the establishment ("Polly, I'm afraid we have abandoned the idea of the topless afternoon teas"), it was nevertheless a wise decision to allow her to dress up a bit more in later episodes. In The Wedding Party the discussion concerning Polly's appearing at the wedding reception in her own 'Jean-Wilson-creation' adds a coquettish and frivolously feminine touch to a world otherwise dominated by Sybil's somewhat 'kitschy' eccentricities and Basil's completely unenchanting, not to say sombre, dress code.

The Ladies, with their roots in a previous century, are characteristically to be seen in dark Edwardian dresses and veiled hats adorned with necklaces, pearls and miscellaneous jewellery. Manuel has, in marked contrast to his difficulties in learning the English language, adopted a distinctive British style of dress, and prefers to walk around in woolly cardigans when not on duty. Terry, of course, wears his chef's jacket practically all the time.

The only clothes that can really be termed casual (Sybil's golf outfit – yellow trousers, yellow shirt, blue jacket and white cape – and the dress of certain obvious proletarians excepted) are Mr. Johnson's leather trousers and strikingly yellow shirt, the latter open all the way down to the waist. The great majority of male hotel guests, however, is correctly dressed in suits and, more often than not, exuberant ties. Alan's bright jacket and open shirt in The Wedding Party are exceptions to the rule, partly explainable by his relative youth, partly by the heat of a summer evening so conducive to amorous escapades and aphrodisiac stimulants, all of which has prompted Mrs. Peignoir to slip into something more comfortable – the same Mrs. Peignoir who later tries her luck again with Basil, by appearing in a dress proudly announcing the colours of the French *drapeau*.

Not really part of the clothing but nevertheless a salient element of personality, is the truly impressive array of moustaches featured in the shows. Apart from Basil himself, wearing John Cleese's own authentic upper lip decoration, Manuel has also been endowed with an amazing concentration of hair under his nostrils. The idea apparently was Andrew Sachs's own, and he had some anxiety that Cleese would take offence. As the latter seemed to ignore this act of insidious mimicry, Sachs decided to keep the protuberance and it eventually became an inalienable part of his character, as well as of the series, in much the same way as the painted moustache of Groucho became a distinct hallmark of the Marx Brothers' films by and large. Perhaps the most impressive gathering of moustaches is otherwise to be found in The Hotel Inspectors, where not only Manuel and Basil flamboyantly flash theirs, but where also Mr. Hutchison 'megalomaniacally' sports a classic Adolf H. rug and Mr. Walt on occasion takes refuge behind the thicket of his massive hedge.

Among the more Latin-inspired 'tango flower beds,' the Major's elegant, perennial sub-nostrilous growth should be emphasised along with the slim hairy line belonging to Gourmet Night's cross Colonel Twitchen. On the other hand, beards in no way have a comparable status and importance inside the Towers. As a matter of fact, I can only think of one character who carries one, and that is the "orelly man" referred to as Lurphy, who, through the intermediary of Manuel, receives the dubious distinction of being named a "hideous ourang-utang" by Basil.

# THE SCRIPTS 7

THE SCRIPTS OF FAWLTY Towers would of course never have made sense without their principal agent, John Cleese. It is impossible even to try to see somebody else in the role of Basil. He is pure typecasting, the blueprint of a genie who has "reacted with the cork and gone bad". It is almost as hard to imagine what the series would have been like without Andrew Sachs or Prunella Scales. In fact, the casting from the very beginning turned out to be a miracle of good fortune. All main characters, that is, those appearing in all or almost all episodes, perform simply marvellously together. Prunella Scales as the dragon wife is so uncannily perfect that it is almost impossible to imagine her as being at all different in private life. Ballard Berkeley, as the dotty Major, is the absolute epitome of a thousand old India hands who stroll the homely boulevards of Cheltenham and Budleigh Salterton. Connie Booth, with her rare gift of being able at the same time to panic and yet remain in command of the situation, is unsurpassable as maid-of-all-work and Basil's catcher in the rye. The two maiden Ladies unforgettably represent those thousands of dear twittery aunts who seem to form the largest segment of the populations of such blameless towns as Harrogate and Torquay itself, and Brian Hall, as Terry, the chef of the second series, though occasionally dangerously close to performing school theatre, nevertheless impresses himself firmly upon the production by virtue of his vigour and enthusiam.

However, since this chapter deals with the script and not with its actual realisation, I must now propose that we distance ourselves as far as we possibly can from the vivid memory images these remarkable actors created, and regard the script as an independent entity, existing prior to its physical realisation at their hands. In other words, we shall try to take a look at how this extraordinary representation of reality was first created in the abstract by its congenial spiritual parents, John Cleese and Connie Booth.

One of the prominent traits of great drama, and by extension great entertainment, is its capability to present simultaneously its subject matter on different levels of abstraction, in this way catering not only to audiences of various ages and educational backgrounds, but also to successive generations and the specific experiences and problems pertaining to their age and era. Thus, great drama is capable of treating a subject in such a way that it both conveys the individual and general aspects of the matter at hand, thereby adapting itself to the changes of time and circumstances. Another of its salient features is that it always lets the person speaking be in the right, meaning that the author does not judge his characters, but lets their actions speak for, or against, themselves.

I dare say that these characteristics apply to Fawlty Towers as well, and that at script level alone it contains more and deeper insights, more profound psychological and social observation, indeed more and deeper esoteric correspondences, than even its creators could have imagined and hoped for. Of course, I do not wish to imply that their conscious intentions can in any way be neglected or even overrated. And I do believe that both Connie Booth and John Cleese were at bottom intensely aware, that by transcending the personal limitations of their own relationship, they were actually furnishing themselves with a remarkably effective divorce therapy. In this way their personal drama was transfigured into something universal.

One thing that will for ever distinguish Fawlty Towers, is that it was from the very beginning a joint venture. It is easy to assess the tremendous impact Cleese's powerful personality had on the creative process. Inversely it is only a bit too easy to overlook the absolute indispensability of Connie Booth. But a quick look at how female psychology features in the series should be enough to convince us that there is more than just average insight into how women really function behind the creation of such characters as Sybil, Polly and the Ladies. To make a person like Sybil emerge from the woodwork of standardised male prejudice and caricature clearly demanded a psychological understanding of rare subtlety and finesse. No matter how impressive Cleese's own talent, alone he could never have created a Sybil that matched Basil so perfectly. It is rather uncanny to see how tuned in she is to all his weaknesses; she has a perfect pitch for every nuance in his mood swings. And just as much as she sees and divines his fears and wishes, she is determined not to care a tinker's cuss about them, as *she* is the one feeling hurt and fundamentally ill treated – I wonder if the devil's grandmother even knew as much about female psychology as 'the mind' that created Sybil! And as I said, a good part of the credit for an achievement so outstanding must rightfully go to Connie Booth.

The amount of sheer everyday realism in Fawlty Towers – as opposed to the general craziness, not to say absurdity of an average Monty Python production – likewise helps convince us that there must have been a serious attempt on the part of the writers to offer the spectators a mirror in which they could easily see and recognise themselves. The outrageousness of Basil – in all likelihood a irresistible temptation for Cleese – was in a most ingenious way tempered and so to speak framed by the 'sound sense of normality' innate in Connie Booth herself. Invariably she turned the script into a solid receptacle for the highly volatile essence it contained: the flamboyant insanity of Cleese's genius. She restrained him and simultaneously made the whole thing credible as a salient example of everyday hell. This curse of normality, this horrror of a perfectly commonplace dull existence facing imminent madness, has paradoxically proved to be the very life elixir of the Towers. Not the least thanks to her graceful touch of placidity, Booth contributed a much-needed counterpoint to the high points in the script and the paroxysms in characterisation. Although the importance of her personality and work will always be in the nature of moonlight compared to the exploding star itself, it will, once the detonation has had time to abate, shine through and illuminate the background of the edifice. Her role was not to be the strings and the bow, but she provided the sound box, without which the great soloist would have remained muted and subdued, no matter how hard he tried to make himself seen and heard.

This said, I maintain that Cleese and Booth here united to form an entity which is more than just the sum total of their personalities and talents. Notwithstanding that their conscious aim certainly was to create comedy pure and simple, what they saw, even could see of its serious implications, was just the tip of the iceberg. By circumnavigating and investigating it at close range we have moved, and continue to move, toward a deeper understanding of this titanic threat to marital happiness. Through painstaking personal experience, we are in fact about to confirm that the wealth of psychological and philosophical material flowing from their horn of plenty is not just to be labelled comedy and entertainment: it is *a frightening vision of reality*. Let me immediately add that I find truly mysterious their ability to transcend the realm of solid boredom inherent in any failing relationship and climb the ladder leading to the sublime. But even in moments when their humour soars in lofty abstractions, there is always a link to a terrestrial substrate, e.g. a solid layer of everyday reality in which the beanstalk is firmly planted. This is all as it should be, because it is at the precise point where heaven and earth meet, that the human comedy is ignited and begins to sparkle.

Comedy in general can be divided into two main categories: the physical and the intellectual. Silent film comedy was almost entirely built upon the down-to-earth attitude of the former, which in western Europe probably originated in the medieval jester, developed into the harlequin or the silently weeping pierrot, eventually to become the mimetic clown of the circus arena. Actors such as Charlie Chaplin, Buster Keaton and Laurel and Hardy were all clowns, obliged to turn their jokes into visual gags. With the advent of spoken film dialogue, humour became verbal too, using dialogue in which we find puns and word-games of all kinds.[22]

The Marx Brothers were among the first successfully to combine in their films vaudeville and slapstick on the one hand and on the other intellectual jokes that were often directly derived from the treasury of Jewish wit and situation comedy. Jewish humour is actually rather hard to define – as in fact is humour in general. But whatever it is, it has been omnipresent in film and television comedy since the early days of Chaplin up to present-day work of

---

[22] One of John Cleese's early influences in the realm of purely verbal entertainment was the radio series *The Goons*, which was broadcast in the U.K. during the 1950s. Although accessible to and admired by general audiences, the series nevertheless featured a subtle, not always obvious kind of humour, which made a particular impression on Cleese, who, some eye witnesses claim, used to laugh at jokes that most other people failed to comprehend, or simply did not consider funny at all.

Woody Allen and Jerry Seinfeld. And we, the audience, never tire of it. Its most typical feature is the paradox: "I could never join a club that would accept me as a member" (Groucho Marx); "For that kind of money, I could have started working yesterday" (Chico Marx); "Don't denigrate masturbation – it's at least making love to someone you really like" (Woody Allen); A: "But you can't fire me; I hardly even work here." B: "That makes it even more difficult." (Seinfeld).

Humour takes someone by surprise, but instead of making him afraid, makes him laugh. A joke that can be anticipated by the audience ceases in most instances to be a joke. This is a fairly general rule, because, even when it is part of a joke's design to create anticipation, we still wonder in which direction it proposes to take us. Tommy Cooper in particular, who died on stage in 'the act of his life', relied primarily on anticipation and its potential of suspense.

It's impossible to define what makes one thing funny and another not funny at all – luckily. So why do I try? Because you are the worshipper and I am your companion, and in this chapter we are dealing with the subtleties of Holy Writ. So if the Fawltys are the twin towers of the cathedral, then the text is the bible, and as such in need of theological exegesis. And, as is the case with the Christian church, the edifice of modern humour has a Jewish foundation.

That the authors of Fawlty Towers were influenced by the Marx Brothers is evident, and at one point tacitly acknowledged, "I'm not doing it. You want to be in a Marx Brothers film, that's your problem. I'm not interested" (The Anniversary). Like the Marx Brothers' work, Fawlty Towers contains a lot of crazy humour and complementary physical action – action requiring perfect body-control and a fine sense of timing. Again, as with the Marx Brothers, the series features some highly intellectual humour – in fact, to understand all its implications is really to gain a sense of spiritual and verbal superiority over one's fellow men ... The main characteristic of this intellectual kind of humour is a multi-faceted play on words (which is the reason that any dubbed version of Fawlty Towers must be an absurdity).

A closer perusal of the scripts reveals that every single episode features a large number of linguistic games, puns, word-plays, onomatopoeic attempts to translate one language into another. (See for instance how Basil's impromptu translation of German into English, "Wir wollen ein Auto mieten" - "we would like to rent a car" – becomes, "I see, you volunteer to go out and buy meat.") There are also misunderstandings arising from different characters investing the same words with different meanings, from general confusion created by words not properly uttered, or deliberately distorted, or deceptively pronounced, or pronounced in the temporary absence of the listener, so as to fatally change the latter's perception of the given context. In short, the essential intellectual device employed by the scriptwriters is: *verbal misunderstanding inevitably leading to a breakdown of communication.*

Particularly characteristic of this phenomenon is the episode in which verbal misapprehension is explicit, namely, Communication Problems. The deaf Mrs. Richards refuses to turn on her hearing aid, and, in consequence, gets practically every verbal message wrong. In a significant way this makes her a symbol of Fawlty Towers in general. Her absolute rock-solid self-assurance in the midst of roaring hurricane *Basil* could tempt one to associate with the eye of the storm, which itself, by reason of its stability, defines the whirling madness around it. In a figurative sense, the essence of this static, imperturbable nucleus could thus be expressed by the equation: *Fawlty Towers = Communication Problems.*

In a most congenial way, the major themes of the entire series are comprised in this one episode. We have S:t George, patron saint of England, we have the old dragon, we have Basil's desperate hope for a better future, we have the staff and the guests caught up in confusion and misunderstanding initiated by a series of false allegations. Above all, we have Sybil's ultimate triumph and Basil's terminal humiliation. (Sybil: "If I find out the money on that horse was yours, you know what I'll do, Basil." Basil: "You'll have to sew 'em back on first.")

The development of the tragedy from its first deceitful glimmers of light ("There is a very nice little filly running at Exeter this afternoon, Mr. Fawlty."), to the downfall of the hero at the hands of immortals, indifferent to human happiness and human despair, is as compelling as that of any of Euripides' plays. This parallel with classical tragedy should not however be over-indulged. As opposed to Greek tragedy, in which the action is set in motion by the chorus, or more rarely by the principal actors, any given Towers episode characteristically begins *in medias res*. We are introduced into an ongoing action with a number of people present.

In A Touch of Class, for instance, we are soon privy to the first typical pun and its typical concomitant confusion. Basil: "There's too much butter *on those trays.*" Manuel: "No, no Senor – *uno, dos, tres.*" From there we are led on to the play on the Italian word for butter (*burro*) which in Spanish means donkey. (This is to become a common verbal ploy throughout the series – Manuel and Basil soon exhaust their meagre stock of words of each other's languages). And very quickly the intellectual content of the scene (on those trays – *uno, dos, tres*) degenerates into onomatopoeic babble. Manuel: "Burro is iiii-aaaa."

Linguistic confusion is at the heart of every scene in which Basil is depicted as the white man and Manuel as his burden. ("Please, understand, before one of us dies!" Communication Problems.) Or consider the scene in which Basil tries to explain that there are two dead pigeons in the water tank, and Manuel instead forms the impression that it contains two flying piglets. Incidentally, this sort of incomprehension leads Basil to associate Manuel's language skills with those of uneducated coolies – *pigeon* becomes *pidgin*, "like your English." (Basil the Rat.)

The linguistic problems that bedevil the relationship between Basil and the Major are different in kind, but equally capable of creating confusion. The Major, a little hard of hearing and perhaps a touch more than just a little senile, misinterprets most of what Basil says with a sort of benevolent inconsequentiality as he wanders off. (The Major: "She's a fine woman, Mrs. Fawlty". Basil: "No, no, I wouldn't say that". The Major: "No, nor would I.")

In those rare moments of interaction between Basil and the Major in which the latter is portrayed as being a little more alert, puns and illogical deductions rather than plain dottiness play a decisive role in creating misunderstandings.

*Basil: No Germans staying this week, Major ... may I have the gun?*

*The Major: But they are animals ... they spread disease, Fawlty ... he was sitting there, eating the nuts, if you please.*

*Basil: What did you say it was?*

*The Major: A vermin* (pronounced with a thick 'i', almost like an a) *a dirty rat ..."*

Another well-constructed dialogue is that initiated by the Major on the difference between Indian and West Indian cricketers. The argument insidiously confounds women with infantile pagans.

*Basil: They do get awfully confused, don't they? They're not thinkers. I see it with Sybil every day.*

*The Major: I do wish I could remember her name* (the woman he invited to see the game). *She's still got my wallet.*

*Basil:* (cutting the Major short) *As I was saying, no capacity for logical thought.*

*The Major: Who?*

*Basil: Women.*

*The Major: Oh yes, yes ... I thought you meant the Indians.*

*Basil: No, no, no, no ... wasn't it Oscar Wilde who said: 'They have brains like Swiss cheese?'*

*The Major: What do you mean – hard?*

*Basil: No, no – full of holes.*

*The Major: Really? ... Indians?*

*Basil: No, women!*

*The Major: Oh.*

The word-play designed for Polly and Basil usually has a different *raison d'être*, and typically takes the form of intimate codes dictated by a sudden sense of urgency, not to say emergency. Basil: "Oh, I see. Oh, (you have come to collect) Mr. Leeman!" Polly: (knowing that Basil is desperate for time) "We thought you said (that you had come to collect) the linen". Basil: (happily surprised and a little bit too loudly) "Brilliant!"

183

Some of the series' more banal puns have actually been put in Polly's mouth in dialogue where they over-saturate the context with associative 'meaning.' Mrs. Arrad: (calling Basil) "Excuse me. There's sugar in the salt-cellar." Basil: "Anything else?" Mrs. Arrad: "I've just put it all over the plaice?" Basil: "What were you doing with it all over the place?" Mrs. Arrad: "All over the *plaice*." (Waldorf Salad.) Here the pun should have been cut short, because the point has been made. The script however has Polly go on, "What a sweet plaice." "Basil: "What?" Polly: (making things even worse) "I'll have it re-placed." The pun is now over-extended, and ready to collapse under its own weight.

Gourmet Night seems to me, and not only because of the above-mentioned blunder, weak in both dialogue and dramatic artifice – it's the one episode in the whole canon that invariably gives me the creeps. Although the theme in itself has a lot of potential, it permits of surprisingly lame and outdated slapstick. (Colonel Hall: "There's a hair in my mousse." Polly: "Well, don't talk too loud or everybody will want one.")

In spite of intermittent well-written scenes, there are other weak points in the dialogue. For instance, Basil: (to Colonel Hall) "How's that lovely daughter of yours?" Sybil, hissing in his ear "She's dead." This rather trite joke that unfortunately colours the rest of the scene. Still, by way of compensation, there's Basil's brilliant remark to the very short, but standing Mrs. Hall: "Oh, sorry! Didn't see you down there. Don't get up." Not to speak of the well-found "Two (too!) small and dry."

The scene in which Basil is supposed to introduce Mr. and Mrs. Twitchen to the Halls is not dramatically convincing, because the viewer has not been alerted as to why the Twitchens, after almost a minute of unforgiving silence, won't help Basil out of his dilemma. As it is, Mr. and Mrs. Twitchen are both obliged to act in a very unnatural way, thus reminding the audience that what they see is not just happening naturally but is the result of a written script.

In the same way, Polly's paraphrases ("he's potted the shrimp," "soused the herring," "pickled the onions," etc.) intended to catch Basil's attention and inform him of the chef's lamentable condition without the guests catching on, lack a certain vivacity. A redeeming quality in this scene, however, is her expression when alluding to the fact that the gourmet chef, Kurt, who has developed an unreciprocated passion for Manuel, is lying dead-drunk under the table. But that really has little to do with humour, and so much more to do with, ahem – sex.

Kurt's literal puking over the mullet is too gross for me. Cleese's comparatively long absence from the action in the dining-room also makes it painfully clear that everything in the series hinges on his presence. Finally, Sybil's role here lacks motivation and consistency, the reason being that the very essence of her relationship with Basil consists of her spitting verbal acid over him whenever he messes things up. In this episode, she's vehemently on the attack right from the beginning, although ostensibly he's done nothing to start her off. This point of departure is not particularly valid, especially as Basil is not on this occasion the cause of everything going wrong.

The action is usually centred on Basil's and Sybil's marital problems, which constitute an excellent platform for all sorts of intellectual and ironic play. In this episode the central conflict is minimised to point up a common problem. Sybil cannot give full play to her sarcasm in this context, and Basil in turn is too busy with guests and staff to retaliate.

So, although there are some incomparable gems in Gourmet Night (Basil's assault on the car, for example), both the script itself and the overall dramaturgy are relatively poor. I take this as proof that the Ladies and the Major represent very important secondary roles. They do appear in the show, but too briefly, and André,

Kurt, and the four dinner guests are all unfamiliar to us. The predominance of new over established characters is disproportionate, and deprives the emerging catastrophe of some of its familiar and much-loved attributes.

However, in pronouncing this critique of Gourmet Night, I do not wish to imply that the Fawlty Towers aficionado should ignore the secret value and meaning of this painful initiation. The episode is an ordeal, but so was the crucifixion of Christ. In the alleged context of twelve unalterable and holy episodes, its function is that of Judas. And without Judas, there is no divine drama, no intense suffering and no final redemption.

John Cleese himself must have been aware of the crucial importance of this one turkey. He is reported to have said, that of all the scenes from the series, the one that today pleases him the most is the one in which he completely demolishes the trifle in search of the lost bird. Why Cleese should have chosen this particular scene I do not know. But then again – who am I to judge the secret workings of a universal drama whose final curtain falls on Sybil's sublime, "I'm afraid it's started to rain again," (Basil the Rat.)

But if some of the puns in Gourmet Night are comparatively weak, there are many other episodes in which they positively shine. One example is this piece of word-play from the beginning of The Hotel Inspectors. Sybil has just shown Basil the box on which the word 'pens' has been written. Sybil: "Well, when Ben comes, you can give them to him." The difference between this and Polly's plays on 'plaice' and 'place' is that Sybil's comment is not a simple homonym, but conceals a biting sideswipe at Basil. The verbal proximity of pens and Ben's is moved forward into a long argument, at the end of which Basil imperiously declares to Mr. Walt that 'P-off' (short for 'piss off!') is an accepted abbreviation of Post Office.

Puns are not the only impediments to communication. An-

other much-employed device is the temporary lapse of attention that leads straight to fateful misunderstanding. This is the case in The Psychiatrist, where Basil hears only the second half of the question featuring "holiday" and "how often can you and your wife manage it?" A similar ploy is used in the scene in which the Major is talking to the moose's head, not realising that the moose's voice is in reality Manuel's from below the counter (The Germans). The Major is led to infer that the head has within it some hidden recorder which enables it to speak and to enter into conversation. The Major, visibly shaken by the amount of surprisingly accurate statements from the head, feels compelled to air his stupefaction to Basil: "I say, that's a remarkable animal, Fawlty. Where did you get it?" Basil: "Sampsons, in the town." The Major: "Japanese, was it?" Basil: " … Canadian, I think." The Major: "I didn't know the Canadians were as clever as that." Which may be taken to show that the Major is indeed about to enter his second childhood, though perhaps not quite in the way Basil imagines it.

But even scenes saturated with both physical and verbal confusion (for instance, "I was talking to you but looking at her" between Basil, Polly and Hutchison in The Hotel Inspectors) are still subject to a dramatic logic which prevents the shows from losing narrative momentum, and so transform into a mere parade of internally unrelated sketches. This is the case with so many Monty Python jokes, which were necessarily short-lived, not least because it was their prime function not to follow conventional rules of narration or to create drama proper. Fawlty Towers is by contrast set in an everyday environment that has been specifically created to have all the appearance of 'reality'. There is a facade of normality, of respectability. As opposed to a Monty Python sketch, a typical Towers episode is not crazy and absurd from the word go, but becomes so through the relentless action provoking Basil out of his precariously maintained composure to full-fledged madness. The various ways in which this dramatic tension inexorably mounts and is orchestrated together with the actors, testify to the meticulous organizational work that went into the creation of the series.

From a dramaturgical point of view, the most atypical of all these crescendi are those featured in The Germans. Where most episodes would centre on one principal theme and outline its ramifications, we see here that there are three quite distinct unities of action. It is structurally the most complex of all the episodes and the final solution (which must not be mentioned!) is the end result of two points of culmination. The first of these is Basil's farewell to his wife at the hospital ("Quite painful, right?"), the second the "nasty knock" from the fire extinguisher. The relation between the moose head and the closing line, ironically uttered by one of their number – "However did they win?" – shows that the German guests weren't, after all, completely dumbfounded by Basil's rambling. They obviously not only knew what he was talking about, but also had their own opinions about what went wrong with the war. Sybil, 'voodooing' the moose's head telekinetically, knocks out her husband once and for all, and, as usual, gets the better of him, while the Major and Manuel themselves have no idea what's going on. The animal's head has been the subject of Sybil's hatred from the very beginning (it did snag her cardies, didn't it?). It is forced to become subservient to her will and is, in fact, the one responsible for running the hotel in her absence.

Basil's inability to control his own behaviour was at the root of the conflict in The Germans. Another way of triggering his mania is to have him jumping to conclusions. In many instances there is no initial verbal misunderstanding, but an interpretation, in itself correct, of a given statement, leads to a highly imaginative leap of misapprehension. A spectacular series of such hasty deductions can be found in The Wedding Party. The point of departure for what is to become one of Basil's wildest, physically as well as mentally exhausting fantasies, is young Alan's asking Basil if the chemist's shop (drugstore) is still open. Already prejudiced against them by his impression that the young couple are enjoying each others' company a little bit too much, and also by his subsequent humiliation at Sybil's hands, Basil is not very much inclined to help his guest. And when it finally dawns upon him that it was naive to assume that Alan wanted prophylactics – he in fact needs some batteries – Basil's imagination runs wild.

The vigour of his crusade against sexual pleasure has been fully demonstrated elsewhere in this book. Here we are concerned about how, in technical and dramatic terms, the ultimate expression of his phobia is achieved. The apparent point of departure is an erroneous conclusion based on a valid premise (both parties now know that it's batteries Alan wants). But although Basil is ashamed of his behaviour – once he has realised his mistake – he is still unable to check the natural course of his libido. It continues to flow through the breach in the dam.

Basil's dialogue with Mrs. Peignoir later in this episode is conspicuously rich in erotic innuendo too. The lady magnifies the sexual explicitness of her part of the conversation by (unintentionally?) making equivocal use of some English words.

*Mrs. Peignoir: You left it* (the tape recorder) *in my room so that you could come and get it, didn't you?*

*Basil: Ha, ha, ha!*

*Mrs. Peignoir:* (coquettishly) *I'm not having you knocking on my door in the middle of the night!* (A line which must be interpreted against the background of Basil's remark in the earlier bedroom scene – the one in which he is seen reading *Jaws*. The doorbell rings. Basil, rehearsing his lines, *Welcome to Basil Fawlty Knocking Shops Limited.*)

*Basil:* (hysterically) *Ha, ha, ha, ha, ha … I should cocoa!*

*Mrs. Peignoir: You naughty man! Good night.*

Which brings us to the grand finale. Mrs. Peignoir's words have rooted themselves in Basil's unconscious at such a depth that he cannot even hear the difference between Sybil's and her voices, though it would take near-deafness not to do so. Throughout the episode Basil has been constant prey to his own erroneous conclusions, conferring motives on other people that they do not in reality have. Taking everything at face value, he is now convinced – maybe not altogether without reason! – that if he had let Mrs. Peignoir have her own way, they might now be together *au naturel* in the lady's bed. The final clash of fantasy and reality is Sybil's sledgehammer wake-up call. And it does not make it any easier for

Basil to distinguish between the one and the other when Sybil herself makes the wrong inference from Manuel's moaning in the kitchen, and tells Basil that there is a burglar in the basement. "We've been to a wedding ..." Curtain!

In itself, the idea of characters mistaking one person for another, or pretending to be other people, is an age-old comic conceit – one finds the device employed over and over again in the classical comedy of Molière, Holberg and others. In Fawlty Towers the supposedly ill and puffy-faced Sybil is impersonated by a reluctant Polly. But in an extended sense, mistaking a person for someone else is an almost instinctive reaction on Basil's part, and a major source of ensuing conflict.

There are basically two methods by way of which the dramatic tension peculiar to the Towers reaches its painful climax. One leads up to a fatal peripeteia (turning point) about midway into the drama, where the dreaded and semi-foreseen catastrophe becomes incontrovertible fact, so that every effort must be made in the way of damage-limitation to prevent total havoc. (See for instance Basil's hectic 'second half' activity in The Builders, The Anniversary and The Kipper and the Corpse). The second entails a race against all odds to avoid a cataclysm at the end of the road. (The Hotel Inspectors, Communication Problems, Gourmet Night and, of course, Basil the Rat.)

This latter episode is particularly revealing – a brilliant example of the mastery and maturity of dramatic purpose and style that the series had acquired at the very moment of its termination ... In this episode the two modes of creating dramatic tension and final release are combined. The peripeteia occurs at the moment when even Basil realises that the rat, his namesake, is loose on the premises – "Well, let's have a little Basil hunt, shall we, and then we'll deal with the sackings later on!" The final cataclysm would surely have been that the health inspector actually finds the "filigree" hamster

191

on his dining table. Both prophecies are fulfilled, but there is one redeeming quality: IT WASN'T REALLY BASIL'S FAULT THAT THE RAT GOT LOOSE IN THE FIRST PLACE!

Significantly, and perhaps surprisingly, Basil the Rat ends on a rather happy note. All the Tower's denizens join forces to avert the impending death-sentence (there is a definite risk that the hotel would have to close down for good were the health inspector to detect a rat loose on the premises). As they succeed in this – somehow – we might assume that the health inspector will not recover from his torpor until it has become too late for him to make further inquiries into what he actually did see inside the biscuit tin. It is as if all the inhabitants of the Towers are determined to seal the last moment of their imaginary existences with sphinx-like smiles as they pronounce in unison: "All the world's a stage, and all the men and women merely players."

In spite of the agonising drama and the intense psychological distress pervading the series, the putative last episode almost seemed to confirm what the American producers of a transatlantic sequel had hoped to convey to their modern unprejudiced audiences, namely that the people in the show were, after all, "all right folks" … Luckily such is not the case. Basil the Rat was only the last episode to be televised, not the last to be produced. In great secrecy a thirteenth episode was written and filmed during the autumn of 1979. It was meant to be the first in a new series of six shows, but its real fate was to become the last episode of all. Considering its ominous title, this is none too surprising. It was named The Robbers.

How can it be?
My wife isn't talking to it...
That usually
staunches it...

# THE THIRTEENTH EPISODE

# 8

In 1999 I visited London for various purposes of little or no interest to my readers. There was however one encounter during the course of the visit that changed my life, and may from now on change the lives of other people too. I had gone to The Red Parrot pub in Piccadilly to meet some friends I hadn't seen in years. We found each other as congenial as ever, and competed in downing beverages of every possible kind and description. I remembered an old Monty Python sketch in which the gang orders drinks made from live animals liquidised in a household mixer. I recalled that one of the drinks was called a 'Harlem Stinger'. An unknown member of the Python species opted for something less 'ducky', and someone then quenched his carnivorous thirst by ordering two Harlem Stingers, taking the precaution to ask the bartender to go easy on the lemming …

Animated discussion of the Pythons eventually led us to the subject of Cleese and Fawlty Towers, and I observed that it was a great pity that there were never more than the twelve episodes. One of my friends replied, "Oh, but that's not true. There's at least one more episode." "You're kidding me," I said, and simply refused to believe him. "Well, let me prove it to you then," he replied, taking out his cellular phone. After talking for a minute, he put the telephone back in his pocket, and said, "He's coming."

This was how I came to meet the BBC's former Public Relations Manager William G. Morton. He had been employed by the BBC in the late 1980s, working his way through the film archive and the library to a position as an assistant editor, before becoming head of the PR department. The fabulous story he had to tell went all the way back to the early days of his apprenticeship, deep down in the air-conditioned media catacombs, where he was registering production data and storing films in endless rows.

One day he was charged with the task of transferring the entire Fawlty Towers series from one part of the archives to another, and with the official computer registration of this transportation as well. Among other things he had to count the numbers of reels and cassettes, and make sure that all the films really were where they were supposed to be. When he took up one of the films to check that it contained number 12, The Hotel Inspectors, he suddenly experienced a powerful impulse to watch it. He did so, came to the end of the film, and was just about to turn the machine off, when he noticed that the music started to pick up again, and the hotel sign was shown, this time reading "Slutty Bowels".

He was utterly astonished. What followed wasn't just a trailer or odds and ends of previous shooting sessions. After The Hotel Inspectors the film simply continued with an entire thirteenth episode. He told his superiors about his find, but nobody seemed to want to talk about it. He finally heard from the Transcription Service that all rights for the series now resided with John Cleese and Connie Booth, and that as far as the BBC were concerned, the contract with the Cleese-Booth Foundation specified the broadcasting of twelve named episodes, no more, no fewer.

But there is one more show, William insisted. Whereupon the definitive answer came, "If we have it in our archives it shouldn't be there. We don't own the rights, and it should be removed." Before anybody else could ensure that these orders were carried out,

William cut the film out and smuggled it through security when he went home that same evening.

That November evening in 1999, we were all invited to his flat. Here I saw the thirteenth episode of Fawlty Towers in its entirety – an absolutely spectacular, cut version that lasted for a good forty-five minutes. We were all speechless after that. It was like seeing the holy grail come into tangible existence. It was a truly wonderful episode, the quintessence of Fawltyism, marvellously acted and suspended in mid-air, to oblige its audience to go on, to continue building its own Tower ...

With the splendour of that vision, there was even an accompanying script – and don't think for a moment that I didn't try to obtain a copy of the cassette! But William didn't want trouble, and so the filmed version was to remain a secret for a few select people in the world (such as myself!). The script, however, was a different story. Or rather, it was the same story. But I did have the audacity to sneak into his hallway and copy it in his fax machine while he was asleep in some young woman's arms, and had consigned everything else in his flat to the gods and his friends' discretion.

When I think about it, I wonder if perhaps that was the greatest mistake I ever made in my life, not to steal the tape that time. I could have done it. And William wouldn't have noticed until the next morning. But he was a friend of a friend, so I didn't.

The script however, was salvaged and I hereby take the risk of evoking the wrath and vengeance of Bill Morton for having betrayed and used him as a vehicle of my own wicked and unscrupulous ambition.

But what the heck! Because of your timidity, millions of people all over the world has been deprived of the last Basilean dispensation; you have monopolised the holy grail; you have decided to let humankind perish in utter darkness. Well, Bill, I cannot remain a privileged sectarian on that point. My goal is to shed light and to pave the way for the master. In other words: Up yours William! Here it is!

# THE ROBBERS

First of third series. According to the text on the cover, scheduled to be broadcast on January 9, 1980, BBC 2, but never aired. No explanation why.

| | |
|---|---|
| Basil Fawlty | John Cleese |
| Sybil Fawlty | Prunella Scales |
| Manuel | Andrew Sachs |
| Polly | Connie Booth |
| Terry | Brian Hall |
| Major Gowen | Ballard Berkeley |
| Miss Tibbs | Gilly Flower |
| Miss Gatsby | Renée Roberts |
| Mr. Sleece | Jeremy Sutherland |
| Mr. Wickeed | Ron Parsley |
| Mr. Underhill | Clive York |
| Mrs. Underhill | Patty Masham |

(It is shortly before noon. Basil is alone in the hotel lobby.)

*Basil:* (absent-mindedly fingering a small machine, and speaking to himself) *Would you believe it? I mean, what's the bloody point in having an electric razor if it doesn't raze. It's like my wife. The only thing she has to do is to work but she won't. And you can't even throw her away because the batteries that were supposed to make her tick are a threat to life on earth.*

*Sybil:* (from the bar) *Basil!*

*Basil: Yes, dear?*

*Sybil: Have you put that calendar up yet?*

*Basil: Calendar?* (silence) *Not as such, dear, but I shall immediately attend to your heart's desire.* (To himself) *Don't see the point. One year's as rotten as the next.* (Hangs it up and looks for the actual day,) *Hmm, May 25th, the day of S:t Mary Magdalene. Her as well, eh? God knows what Christ saw in her.*

*The Major:* (arriving in the lobby) *Papers arrived yet, Fawlty?*

*Basil: Indeed, Major.*

*The Major:* (reading a headline aloud) *"Thatcher Strikes Back Against Criminality."*

*Basil: Good idea. Pity being a woman can't be made a capital offence.*

*The Major: Well, they aren't all that bad, are they? Think of your wife.*

*Basil: I was just thinking of her, Major. As a Minister she would make Hitler seem like a Boy Scout.*

*The Major: Well, at least Baden Powell wasn't German.*

*Basil: No, thank heaven. They were spared.*

*The Major: Well then, when's the election?*

*Basil: Election?*

*The Major: I understood you to say your wife was running for office.*

*Basil: Only in my private little concentration camp, Major.*

*The Major: Well, I'm sure they'll like her there* (wanders off).

*Sybil:* (entering the office by the back door) *How many times do I have to tell you not to throw used batteries in the waste-paper basket, Basil? They're a threat to Nature.*

*Basil: They're not the only ones.*

*Sybil: Your dirty socks run them pretty close.*

*Basil: Thank you, dear.*

*Sybil: So are you going to remove them?*

*Basil: I'm sorry, but they're fused to my feet.*

*Sybil: The batteries, Basil!*

*Basil: Why don't you do it, since you're nearest?*

*Sybil: Because I'm busy doing the bar inventory.*

*Basil: And in thirty seconds the whisky'll turn sour if you don't order more?*

*Sybil: No, but in half an hour it's lunch, and all the staff from the Prophylactic Emporium will be here for their reunion. And that begins at 11:45 a.m. in the bar.*

*Basil: Oh yes, I'd forgotten. The public announcement will be that thanks to them thousands of women have been able to run away from home and come back with coloured balloons. And now – let's sing along and inflate the lot!*

*Sybil: Oh Basil, don't be so prudish. They pay awfully well because nobody else will have them, and since we have no other bookings today, there'll be nobody except the Major and the Ladies around – they both used to work for them in London, you know.*

*Basil: Yes indeed. I wonder what happened to good old Jack the Ripper. A great service to society, he was.*

*Sybil: It's business, Basil.*

*Basil:* (to himself) *Yet they insist on calling it marriage.*

(Basil leaves, and returns with the batteries in one hand. Two rather rough and vulgar-looking men, Mr. Wickeed and Mr. Sleece, enter the hotel.)

Basil: Oh, welcome. Go right in. My wife has just stuffed the canapes with birth control pills, and decorated the dining-room with French letters. It's really quite inventive of her.

Mr. Wickeed: We're looking for a room.

Basil: A double, perchance?

Mr. Sleece: Yeah, we sort of want to relax a bit before lunch.

Basil: Don't you have homes in town? Or are you just sleeping on a mattress in the back of your delivery van?

Mr. Wickeed: That's right. And now we would like to be a bit more comfortable, if you see what I mean.

Basil: (curtly) Check-in is at twelve.

Mr. Sleece: We'll pay for the extra day if we can get a room right away.

Basil: But the rooms aren't done yet.

Mr. Sleece: Oh, that don't matter.

Basil: I mean, it is eleven o'clock, just another hour. Well, suit your-selves, if that's what you want, frolicking in other peoples' lice and scabs. I can't believe what the world is coming to … (starting to

204

hand over the form, then suddenly interrupting himself, seized by a suspicion). *On second thoughts, what do you think this is — a red-light flophouse with rooms available by the hour? Of course, I should have known. Judging by your appearance I thought you must be from the YMCA, but now I realise ...*

*Mr. Wickeed:* (impatiently) *What the hell are you talking about?*

*Basil: Don't you dare address me in that tone of voice! You scum, you perverts, you think you can just walk in here as calm as you like and ask for a room so that you can elope from decent society together? Don't you know that you're shunned like lepers all over Torquay? And just because we have the courtesy of allowing your reunion — I mean, I have never ever heard anything so utterly disgusting in my entire life!*

(The two men exchange worried glances, and are about to leave the hotel when Sybil enters from the bar.)

*Sybil: What on earth is going on here, Basil?*

*Basil: I'll tell you what's going on here, my dove. These two mummy's angels just minced in here hand in hand, as if nothing could have been more natural, and asked me to put them up in a double room for an hour.*

*Sybil: Yes? And why didn't you?*

*Basil:* (flabbergasted) *What? Isn't it enough that we have these buggers here for drinks? I'll have to ask Chef to have all the glasses disinfected when they've gone.*

(Mr. Wickeed and Mr. Sleece look at him, totally bewildered.)

*Sybil: Aren't you from the Prophylactic Emporium?*

*Mr. Wickeed: No, no. We just wanted a room, just for the night. We're ... journeying ... through the country ... but I guess, this might be ...*

*Sybil: Not at all. Please stay. We have a nice double room for you, overlooking the sea.*

*Mr. Sleece: But your husband thought we were some ...*

*Sybil: Oh, don't mind him. He wouldn't know a Sunday school teacher from a serial killer on the loose.*

*Basil: Oh, I see, you gentlemen are from the local Sunday school. Heart-rending tales of Jesus among the little boys, eh?*

*Mr. Wickeed: Well, we prefer to see ourselves as charity workers. A bit like Robin Hood, if you see what I mean.*

*Basil:* (with a wolfish grin) *But of course. Tax evasion and all that stuff. That's what they finally got Capone for, wasn't it?*

*Sybil: Manuel!*

*Manuel:* (appearing from the dining-room) *Si? Si, señora.*

*Sybil: Would you please show these gentlemen to room 16.*

*Manuel: Qué?*

*Basil:* (to Manuel) *Number 69, Manuel, jolly good luck with it! See it as a dream come true.*

(Sybil hands over the form for the two men to fill in. When Mr. Sleece with some difficulty begins to write she takes a closer look at his many tattoos, especially the anchor on the right upper arm and the dragon encircling the name Daisy on his chest. She also sees the three tattooed spots in the space between his thumb and index finger.)

*Sybil: Excuse me, but are you by any chance a sailor?*

*Mr. Sleece: I guess you could call me that.*

*Sybil: Oh, I have always dreamt of the freedom of the ocean, the waves, the salty breeze … and those three dots on your hand, what do they actually stand for?*

*Basil: Somewhere between eight and twelve years' worth of prison, I should say.*

*Mr. Sleece:* (ignoring Basil, addressing Sybil with a vulgar leer) *Faith, Hope and Charity.*

*Mr. Wickeed: Especially Charity. Ha ha.*

*Sybil: How romantic, all those seas and harbours …*

*Basil: Gonnorhea Bay, the archipelago of Syphilis, Port Buttocks.*

*Mr. Sleece:* (taking up his wallet, which Basil sees to be full of high-denomination notes) *Oh, yeah, since we might be leaving early tomorrow morning, can we pay in advance?*

*Basil: Absolutely no need. Dressed in lace, black stockings and not much else, my wife will bring you a breakfast tray with fresh roses from the garden at five o'clock in the morning. However, a small tip for any extra services on her part would be appreciated.*

*Sybil:* (after giving Basil a glance that could kill) *Certainly, Mr. Sleece.*

(The two men start up the stairs, carrying a large briefcase between them. Manuel tries to take it from them.)

*Mr. Sleece: No thanks. I'll handle it.*

*Manuel: No, no. Is no problem.*

*Mr. Sleece: I said I'll handle it.*

*Manuel: But is my job!*

(Manuel pulls at the handle of the case. In the ensuing struggle he falls over and rolls down the stairs. The briefcase flies open and Basil, on his way to chastise Manuel, sees that it's full of bank notes. He pretends not to have seen them. Mr. Sleece quickly closes the case, and the two men go upstairs.)

(It is lunchtime in the dining-room. Beside the Ladies and the Major there is another couple and the two men who have just checked into the hotel. Basil has addressed himself to the Major, pretending he has to speak loudly to make himself understood.)

*Basil: … and because of these burglars breaking into the hotel the other day we had to have the police round to rule out the guests as suspects.*

*The Major: Really? Who was it?*

*Basil: It wasn't.*

*The Major: Wasn't? I don't quite follow, Fawlty.*

*Basil: It wasn't one of the guests.*

*The Major: Strange, I really thought I saw one today.*

*Basil: Who did you say?*

*The Major: No, no, not him – another guest.*

*Basil:* (turning to the couple who has overheard and are puzzled by this conversation) *And so we had a safety system installed which puts Fort Knox to shame, if I may say. A real Franz Jaeger.*

*The Major: German bunker, is it, Fawlty?*

*Basil: Straight from Berlin, Major.*

*The Major: Achtung Panzer! Read it in General Patton's autobiography. There were lots of them in Operation Desert Storm too, you know.*

*Mr. Underhill: Could we have some more sauce, please?*

*Basil:* (handing Manuel the sauce-boat) *Manuel, please go and get some more sauce.*

*Manuel: Qué?*

*Basil: Sauce! ... Some more sauce!!*

*Mrs. Underhill: Salsa, por favor.*

(Manuel starts to dance. Basil hits him with the sauce-boat. Manuel runs off into the kitchen.)

*Basil: I'm sorry, but he's from Spain. Actually, a speaking ape from Gibraltar. Terribly rare specimen. Missing link between Cro-Magnon and Neanderthal, really.*

*Mr. Underhill: Oh, we don't mind, we like Spanish people. We go to the Costa del Sol every year for our holidays.*

*Basil:* (to himself, very *sotto voce*) *Riff-raff ...* (aloud) *So, the point is, we can now recommend that anyone who has any valuables deposit them in our new dynamite-, fire- and water-proof safe.*

(Polly comes in with the main courses for Mr. Sleece and Mr. Wickeed, who have followed the conversation with the closest attention.)

*Mr. Sleece: Is it true there have been burglars around here stealing from hotel rooms, then?*

Polly: Yes, but it is all under control now.

Mr. Wickeed: Did they collar them?

Polly: Oh yes, they were brought down to the police station two days ...

Basil: (interrupting her) As a matter of fact, they weren't, Polly.

Polly: But I saw the two men being put in the police van, Mr. Fawlty.

Basil: Oh, I see. You mean the two men that were escorted by the police two days ago. Ahh, those were in fact two guests, charity workers on their way to a conference.

Mr. Sleece: Why would charity workers have police escort?

Basil: Afraid. Afraid of being assaulted.

Mr. Wickeed: Of being assaulted?

Basil: By the local trade union organisation. They'd decided to give them a lesson.

Mr. Sleece: Er, physically?

Basil: Sort of. I mean, a little, enough to set an example, not really hurt them. Still ...

Mr. Wickeed: So the burglars are still on the run?

*Basil: Ahh, I'm afraid that's correct. But not to worry, we have just called the police, and they'll be coming over to search all the rooms again this afternoon.*

*Polly: Search all the rooms again?*

*Basil: Just a precautionary measure, to make sure nothing's left to chance. The police are awfully community-minded here in Torquay. I mean, it's more than their job's worth not to make sure tourism isn't harmed, isn't it? If, on the other hand you might feel that you'd rather not have the police going through your belongings, we can always guarantee their absolute, er, tranquillity in our safe, as I said, real Franz Jaeger. Our discretion is one hundred per cent. No questions asked. Ha ha!*

(Polly gives Basil a bewildered look. The two men glance at each other.)

*Mr. Wickeed: We'd better get out of this madhouse now!*

*Mr. Sleece: Bad idea, mate. If we check out now it'll only seem suspicious, and we'd soon have the police up our arses. God, I even showed my tattoos to that stupid mare. She'll have a perfect description.*

*Mr. Wickeed: What a diabolical piece of luck, some amateurs hanging round for a few pounds sticking out of a handbag.*

*Mr. Sleece: And here's us with the big money thinking this'll do as a safe house for a day or two until the heat's off. It's enough to make a cat laugh.*

*Mr. Wickeed: But, like I said, we've got to be somewhere else when the police come, but it would be too obvious to leave the hotel once we've moved in.*

*Mr. Sleece: What shall we do with the money?*

*Mr. Wickeed: Good question … Hm … hm …Got it, mate! The safest place for the money when the cops come will be that safe. Nobody would look for stolen goods in the hotel's own safe. We'll stash it there!*

*Mr. Sleece: Are you completely off your trolley?*

*Mr. Wickeed: No.*

*Mr. Sleece: So what's next, then?*

*Mr. Wickeed: We collect the briefcase in the morning and check out. And then: Rio de Janeiro! Copacabana! Cuba libres! Women!* (loudly, and making a gesture towards the kitchen region) *Salsa!*

*Mrs. Underhill: Oh, please, have some of ours. We've got plenty.*

(Polly and Terry are talking in the kitchen.)

*Polly: I promise you, Terry, he stood there saying that the thieves hadn't been caught and that the police will be back here this afternoon to go through the rooms once again. And then he was bragging about the safe.*

*Terry: About the safe?*

*Polly: Yes. It was as if he was trying to convince people to put all their things in there. Suitcases – everything!*

*Terry: But he hates locking things in the safe; he always forgets what he's done with the key. Besides, after what happened all that time ago, with that lord who turned out to be an impostor …*

*Manuel:* (looking past the kitchen door towards the lobby) *Psst. Come and see.*

(They all three peep past the door and see Mr. Wickeed and Mr. Sleece slowly moving towards the reception desk in the lobby carrying the briefcase between them. Out of the blue Basil materialises behind the desk, flashing what is intended to be a friendly smile.)

*Basil: Can I be of service to you gentlemen?*

*Mr. Wickeed: We was just a bit worried about what you just said in the dining room, about burglars and stuff, so, well, the thing is that we do have a few papers, of no commercial value, of course, all the same …*

*Basil:* (now beaming) *As I said, we do not investigate the reasons why our guests want to keep their valuables in our safe. Considering the circumstances, I can only congratulate you on your excellent initiative. After all, it isn't so nice to have the police going through all one's dirty laundry, is it? Ha!*

*Mr. Sleece: To be perfectly honest, Mr. Fawlty, of course we are not part of the Robin Hood gang, but insurance salesmen. We trade in people's lives, you see. And we don't want anyone to get hurt by unwelcome publicity, or see their private lives exposed unnecessarily. We're travelling on to Cornwall early tomorrow morning, so if you ...*

*Basil: I absolutely understand. I shall be here personally to make sure your insurance policies are unscathed. Would you like a morning call?*

*Mr. Sleece: No. Just be here at seven o'clock.*

*Basil: My pleasure.*

(From inside the bar, Sybil's seal-being-machine-gunned laughter can be heard above the hum of conversation in the bar, where the staff of the Prophylactic Emporium are having their reunion. Mr. Wickeed and Mr. Sleece look at Basil in wonderment.)

*Basil: My wife. She was born in South Africa. As a child she could kill an impala within shooting range just by laughing at it. Amazing, isn't it?*

(Early next morning in the lobby. Basil, looking spruce, is having a cup of tea at the desk. Mr. Sleece and Mr. Wickeed approach.)

*Basil: Ah, good morning. I see duty calls.*

*Mr. Sleece: Could we have the briefcase?*

*Basil: Absolutely no problem.* (Starts looking for the key in his trouser pockets, goes to his jacket, then back to his trousers; smiles at his guests. He bows down and, surprisingly, comes up with the key in his hand. He gives a histrionic sigh of relief and moves over to the safe. He inserts the key into the lock, struggles to turn it but doesn't manage to open the safe. Mr. Sleece and Mr. Wickeed don't seem to enjoy the show very much.)

*Mr. Sleece:* (menacingly) *Can we help you, Mr. Fawlty?*

*Basil: It's this damned lock. It's brand-new, I mean, if you can't even trust a safe.*

(Mr. Sleece and Mr. Wickeed move in on Basil.)

*Basil: Ah, there you are. Would you like to give it a try yourselves?*

(Mr. Sleece tries to turn the key but gets nowhere. Mr. Wickeed does the same, but it's stuck fast, like the sword in the stone. Basil hands them a wrench to provide more leverage. As Mr. Sleece puts all his weight on the key, it breaks off in the keyhole.)

*Basil: Oh, I'm terribly sorry.*

*Mr. Sleece: You talk too much, cully. Now, open the bleeding safe!*

*Basil: I'm sorry, I can't. We'll have to wait for the locksmith to call. He opens at half past eight. It'll be a piece of cake for him. Why don't you have some breakfast while we're waiting?*

*Mr. Sleece: Listen good, Fawlty, I'm not sure what you're up to. But I do know that the police never showed up yesterday to search the rooms like you said.*

*Basil: Oh, yes, quite right, quite right. They called to say they were looking for some bank robbers who might possibly be in the area, and that they'll be round later. So everything's perfectly all right, really. And as to the rest, we'll compensate you for the delay. And breakfast is on us, of course. Would you care to move into the breakfast-room?*

*Sybil:* (passing through the lobby) *Good morning ... What seems to be the matter?*

*Basil: Nothing, dear.*

*Mr. Sleece: We checked a briefcase in the safe yesterday, and now it seems the key's broken off in the lock.*

*Sybil: The key's broken off?*

*Mr. Wickeed: That's right. And your husband tells us we can't get our case till the locksmith comes, when the police will be all over the place checking the rooms ...*

*Sybil: The police? Checking the rooms? What on earth is going on here?*

*Basil: Nothing, dear. Would you like to try the key yourself? I'll just make sure these gentlemen get their breakfast.* (He goes into the kitchen.)

*Basil:* (enthusiastically) *Good morning, Terry.*

*Terry:* (warily) *Good morning, Mr. Fawlty.*

*Basil:* (even more expansively) *Terry, my good fellow, would you be so kind as to prepare a full breakfast for two. A veritable feast, flowers, champagne – that sort of thing.*

*Terry:* (bewildered) *But we don't have any guests to give it to, Mr. Fawlty, only the regulars.*

*Basil: Well, I have to tell you it's a bit of a special day for me and my wife.*

*Terry: Wedding anniversary, is it, then?*

*Basil: By no means. Ever so much more joyous. Her mother died a year ago today.* (to himself) *... Her turn next ...*

*Terry:* (entering into the spirit of the thing) *In that case, Mr. Fawlty, might I suggest that you gather some flowers from the garden while I have a go at the old omelette with truffles?*

*Basil: I shall be delighted to ... Now, where are the plastic ones?*

(The Major, dressing before his window, sees Sybil struggling to get away from two men who have tied her scarf over her mouth and seem about to make off with her. He rushes down the stairs with his gun, bumps into Polly, and falls over. Polly is holding a note which she has just picked up from the desk in the lobby. She bends over to help the Major up. Meanwhile, Basil has returned from the garden with the flowers for the table.)

Polly: Mr. Fawlty, she's been taken away!

Basil: I know. Splendid, isn't it? But why the excitement? It's a year ago, after all.

Polly: No, no, Mr. Fawlty! Your wife – they've kidnapped your wife!

Basil: Who?

Polly: The men that were here, of course! Look, they've left a ransom note.

(Basil reads the note, pretends that he's having an apoplectic fit, and falls to the ground. As both the Major and Basil are regaining consciousness, Manuel enters from the kitchen.)

Manuel: Mr. Fawlty! Special breakfast for you and Mrs. Fawlty, Mr. Fawlty!

The Major: (sitting up and pointing the gun dangerously in all directions) Where are they?

Polly: They've already gone, Major.

The Major: In India we used to shoot rotters like that on the spot. Without trial, dammit!

Manuel: (at whom the gun is now pointing) Ahh, no. I no do harm. It was the great tiger. (Lets the tray fall. The champagne bottle hits the Major on the head. He is knocked out again.)

*Basil: What now?*

*Polly: Call the police! Manuel, go and get some water to pour over the Major.*

*Manuel: No, no. He want kill me!*

*Polly: He is after the kidnappers, Manuel!*

*Manuel: No, no. Hhhe dangerous.*

(Terry comes with water for the Major as the Ladies appear. Basil is lying full length on the floor, reading the ransom note.)

*Basil: One hundred thousand pounds to return my wife alive.* (starts to sob). *Oh, my dearest, darling Sybil, Sybil, my dove, what have they done to you? How am I ever going to get you back? Uh, uh, uhhh … Sybil, my little piranha!*

*Polly: Mr. Fawlty.*

*Basil: Uhhh, uhhh, uhhh.*

*Polly: You must call the police. Here, take the 'phone.*

*Basil:* (pulling himself together) *I can't do that. They say they'll kill her if the police get involved. They'll do it. These people have no scruples whatsoever.* (He takes a dignified walk around the room, goes to the desk, opens the cash box and starts counting the money in it.) *Polly, I shall call the bank and ask them to hand over our savings for the last fifteen years.* (he strikes a pose)

*Alas, t'will be a mere drop in the ocean. Well, I've got to come up with something. I have* (looks dramatically at his wristwatch) *exactly twenty-four hours.*

*Miss Tibbs: Oh, Mr. Fawlty what a terrible thing! We must help you.*

*Basil: How do you mean?*

*Miss Gatsby: We have money.*

*Miss Tibbs: After all, we are your oldest residents, and we ought to help you. If you go down, we go as well.*

*Basil: Oh, that's most kind of you – but no, I could never accept money from the guests.*

*Miss Tibbs: But it would be a loan, Mr. Fawlty.*

*Miss Gatsby: That's right. Please let us help you, Mr. Fawlty. Your wife is in peril. We have money under our beds.*

*Polly: I'll chip in with all I have.*

*The Major: My pension won't go far, but I'll sell my golf clubs as well.*

*Terry: Mr. Fawlty, we have a duty.*

*Manuel: And I go to pawn shop, leave my matador costume to English ignorants!*

*Basil: It's things like this that make life worth-while. What is a human being worth, I ask you, until put to the test by the grim exigencies of an adverse fate? The nobility and kindness of your hearts touch me beyond mere words. This is the testimony of true loyalty and greatness. Let's get Sybil back, shall we?*
*All the others: Yes!*

(Next morning in the lobby. There is a heap of money on the floor and even bigger stacks of counted banknotes on the desk.)

*Polly:* (gathering the last bills and coins and counting them) *That makes ninety nine thousand, nine hundred and seventy-four pounds and three pence, Mr. Fawlty. We're still sixteen pounds short.*

*Basil:* (goes behind the counter, returning with a pink piggy-bank and a hammer; smashes the pig and counts the money) *That's it. We are actually four pounds up. That should be enough to buy everybody a drink when I get back.* (he strikes an oratorical pose) *Dear friends, I shall be leaving you, but not for long. May I say, it is actions like this that have made England the ruler of the seas and the master of the world. Captain Oates! Sir Philip Sidney! Edith Cavell! And others of that ilk! I shall never forget what you have done for me and my wife today. May God bless you all.*

*Miss Tibbs: God bless you, Mr. Fawlty, and bring her back safely.*

*Basil: Thank you a thousand times. And you, Polly, if anything should happen to me, take good care of my hotel* (kisses her gently on the forehead).

(Basil takes all the money and puts it in his briefcase. They all follow him out to the steps as he walks to the car. Once inside he reaches under the passenger seat. He pulls out the bank robbers' briefcase, opens it and sees with great satisfaction that all the money is still there. He gloats over the money.)

   Basil: (to the money) *God, it's going to be hard to say goodbye to you.*

(An abandoned car-park somewhere outside Torquay. It is still early morning, grey and dreary. A single car can be seen in the distance. Basil moves towards it. As he gets closer its headlights are turned on so as to blind him. He flinches, trying to avoid the glare. Opening his car door he sees the two men armed with guns, with Sybil between them. They remove the scarf from her mouth. There is a moment's pause. Basil's foot is just about to touch the ground when Sybil's voice reaches him.)

   Sybil: *Basil!*

(Quickly the foot is withdrawn. The car spins round. At full speed it leaves the car-park. The two men just stand there, gaping, their guns adroop.

   Sybil: (absolutely hysterical) *Basil! Basil!! Basil!!!*

THE END